From

PORTABLE
Cancún

4th Edition

by David Baird & Juan Cristiano

Here's what the critics say about Frommer's:

"Amazingly easy to use. Very portable, very complete."
—*Booklist*

"Detailed, accurate, and easy-to-read information for all price ranges."
—*Glamour Magazine*

"Hotel information is close to encyclopedic."
—*Des Moines Sunday Register*

"Frommer's Guides have a way of giving you a real feel for a place."
—*Knight Ridder Newspapers*

Wiley Publishing, Inc.

Published by:

WILEY PUBLISHING, INC.

111 River St.
Hoboken, NJ 07030-5774

ISBN: 978-0-470-14572-2

Editor: Maureen Clarke
Production Editor: Jonathan Scott
Cartographer: Anton Crane
Photo Editor: Richard Fox
Anniversary Logo Design: Richard Pacifico
Production by Wiley Indianapolis Composition Services

Front cover photo: Mayan Sand Pyramid.

For information on our other products and services or to obtain technical support, please contact our Customer Care Department within the U.S. at 800/762-2974, outside the U.S. at 317/572-3993 or fax 317/572-4002.

Wiley also publishes its books in a variety of electronic formats. Some content that appears in print may not be available in electronic formats.

Manufactured in the United States of America

5   4   3   2   1

Contents

List of Map

ABOUT THE AUTHORS

David Baird is a writer, editor, and translator who has lived several years in different parts of Mexico. Now based in Austin, Texas, he spends as much time in Mexico as possible.

A resident of Mexico City, **Juan Cristiano** is a native of Los Angeles who has written extensively about destinations in Mexico and Latin America, the United States, and Western Europe.

AN INVITATION TO THE READER

In researching this book, we discovered many wonderful places—hotels, restaurants, shops, and more. We're sure you'll find others. Please tell us about them, so we can share the information with your fellow travelers in upcoming editions. If you were disappointed with a recommendation, we'd love to know that, too. Please write to:

Frommer's Portable Cancún, 4th Edition
Wiley Publishing, Inc. • 111 River St. • Hoboken, NJ 07030-5774

AN ADDITIONAL NOTE

Please be advised that travel information is subject to change at any time—and this is especially true of prices. We therefore suggest that you write or call ahead for confirmation when making your travel plans. The authors, editors, and publisher cannot be held responsible for the experiences of readers while traveling. Your safety is important to us, however, so we encourage you to stay alert and be aware of your surroundings. Keep a close eye on cameras, purses, and wallets, all favorite targets of thieves and pickpockets.

OTHER GREAT GUIDES FOR YOUR TRIP:

Frommer's Spanish PhraseFinder & Dictionary
Frommer's Cancún & the Yucatán Day by Day
Frommer's Cancún, Cozumel & the Yucatán 2008
Frommer's Mexico 2008
Frommer's Portable Acapulco, Ixtapa & Zihuatanejo
Frommer's Portable Los Cabos & Baja
Frommer's Portable Puerto Vallarta, Manzanillo & Guadalajara

FROMMER'S STAR RATINGS, ICONS & ABBREVIATIONS

Every hotel, restaurant, and attraction listing in this guide has been ranked for quality, value, service, amenities, and special features using a **star-rating system.** In country, state, and regional guides, we also rate towns and regions to help you narrow down your choices and budget your time accordingly. Hotels and restaurants are rated on a scale of zero (recommended) to three stars (exceptional). Attractions, shopping, nightlife, towns, and regions are rated according to the following scale: zero stars (recommended), one star (highly recommended), two stars (very highly recommended), and three stars (must-see).

In addition to the star-rating system, we also use **seven feature icons** that point you to the great deals, in-the-know advice, and unique experiences that separate travelers from tourists. Throughout the book, look for:

Finds	Special finds—those places only insiders know about
Fun Fact	Fun facts—details that make travelers more informed and their trips more fun
Kids	Best bets for kids—advice for the whole family
Moments	Special moments—those experiences that memories are made of
Overrated	Places or experiences not worth your time or money
Tips	Insider tips—some great ways to save time and money
Value	Great values—where to get the best deals

The following **abbreviations** are used for credit cards:

AE	American Express	DISC	Discover	V	Visa
DC	Diners Club	MC	MasterCard		

FROMMERS.COM

Now that you have this guidebook to help you plan a great trip, visit our website at **www.frommers.com** for additional travel information on more than 3,600 destinations. We update features regularly to give you instant access to the most current trip-planning information available. At Frommers.com, you'll find scoops on the best airfares, lodging rates, and car rental bargains. You can even book your travel online through our reliable travel booking partners. Other popular features include:

- Online updates of our most popular guidebooks
- Vacation sweepstakes and contest giveaways
- Newsletters highlighting the hottest travel trends
- Online travel message boards with featured travel discussions

Planning Your Trip to Cancún

Cancún remains Mexico's calling card to the world, exquisitely showcasing the country's breathtaking natural beauty as well as the depth of its 1,000-year history. One astonishing statistic suggests that more Americans travel to Cancún than to any other overseas destination. Indeed, nearly three million people visit this enticing beach resort annually—most of them on their first trip to Mexico.

The reasons for Cancún's allure have not changed since the government turned this once-isolated beach into a five-star destination. While it embodies Caribbean splendor and the exotic joys of Mexico, even a traveler feeling apprehensive about visiting foreign soil will feel completely at ease here. Cancún also offers the highest quality accommodations and easy access by air; English is spoken, and dollars are accepted; roads are well-paved and lawns manicured. Most travelers feel comfortable in Cancún, while some also feel surprised to find that it almost resembles a U.S. beach resort more than authentic Mexico.

Despite Cancún's convenience as a destination, a little planning can still make the difference between a good trip and a great one. When should you go? What's the best way to get there? How much should you plan to spend? What safety or health precautions should you take? We'll answer these and other practical questions in this chapter.

1 Orientation

CANCUN LAYOUT

Cancún (or "golden snake" in Mayan) stretches from the old city to a 24km (15-mile) sliver of land connected to the mainland by two bridges. Between the old and the new rests the expansive Nichupté lagoon, a lush reminder of Cancún's jungle past.

There are really two Cancúns: **Isla Cancún (Cancún Island)** and **Ciudad Cancún (Cancún City).** The latter, on the mainland, has restaurants, shops, and less expensive hotels, as well as pharmacies, dentists, automotive shops, banks, travel and airline agencies, and car-rental firms—all within an area about 9 square blocks. The city's

Cancún

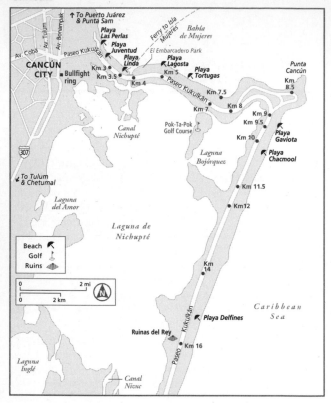

main thoroughfare is **Avenida Tulum.** Heading south, Avenida Tulum becomes the highway to the airport and to Tulum and Chetumal; heading north, it intersects the highway to Mérida and the road to Puerto Juárez and the Isla Mujeres ferries.

The famed **Zona Hotelera,** or Hotel Zone (also called the Zona Turística, or Tourist Zone), stretches out along Isla Cancún, which is a sandy strip 22km (14 miles) long, shaped like a "7." It connects to the mainland by the Playa Linda Bridge at the north end and the Punta Nizuc Bridge at the southern end. Between the two areas lies Laguna Nichupté. Avenida Cobá from Cancún City becomes Bulevar Kukulkán, the island's main traffic artery. Cancún's international airport is just inland from the south end of the island.

Tips **The Best Websites for Cancún**

- **All About Cancún: www.cancunmx.com**   This site is a good place to start planning. There's a database of answers to the most common questions, called "The Online Experts." It's slow, but it has input from lots of recent travelers to the region.

- **Cancún Convention & Visitors Bureau: www.cancun. info**   The official site of the Cancún Convention & Visitors Bureau lists excellent information on events and attractions. Its hotel guide is one of the most complete available, and it has an active message board of recent visitors to Cancún.

- **Cancún Online: www.cancun.com**   This comprehensive guide has lots of information about things to do and see in Cancún, with most details provided by paying advertisers. You can even reserve a tee time or conduct wedding planning online.

- **Cancún Travel Guide: www.go2cancun.com**   This group specializing in online information about Mexico has put together an excellent resource for Cancún rentals, hotels, and attractions. Note that it lists only paying advertisers, but you'll find most of the major players.

- **Mexico Web Cancún Chat: www.mexicoweb.com/chats/ cancun**   This is one of the more active chats online specifically about Cancún. The users share inside information on everything from the cheapest beer to the quality of food at various all-inclusive resorts.

FINDING AN ADDRESS   Cancún's street-numbering system is a holdover from its early days. Addresses are still given by the number of the building lot and by the *manzana* (block) or *supermanzana* (group of blocks). The city is relatively compact, and the downtown commercial section is easy to cover on foot.

On the island, addresses are given by kilometer number on Bulevar Kukulkán or by reference to some well-known location. In Cancún, streets are named after famous Maya cities. Chichén Itzá, Tulum, and Uxmal are the names of the boulevards in Cancún, as well as nearby archaeological sites.

THE SURROUNDING REGION AT A GLANCE

In addition to attractions of its own, Cancún is a convenient distance from the more traditional resorts of Isla Mujeres and the coastal zone now known as the Riviera Maya—extending down from Cancún, through Playa del Carmen, to the Maya ruins at Tulum, Cozumel, Chichén Itzá, and Cobá. All lie within day-trip distance.

Travelers to the peninsula have an opportunity to see pre-Hispanic ruins—such as **Chichén Itzá** and **Tulum**—and the living descendants of the cultures that built them, as well as the ultimate in resort Mexico: **Cancún.** The peninsula borders the aquamarine Gulf of Mexico on the west and north, and the clear blue Caribbean Sea on the east. It covers almost 197,600 sq. km (76,294 sq. miles), with nearly 1,600km (1,000 miles) of shoreline. Underground rivers and natural wells called *cenotes* are a peculiar feature of this region.

2 Visitor Information & Maps

The **State Tourism Office,** Cancún Center, Bulevar Kukulkán Km 9, 1st floor, Zona Hotelera (© **998/881-9000;** www.qroo.gob.mx), is open Monday to Friday from 9am to 8pm. The **Cancún Municipal Tourism Office** is downtown on Avenida Cobá at Avenida Tulum (© **998/887-3379**). It's open Monday through Friday from 9am to 7pm. Each office lists hotels and their rates, and ferry schedules. For information prior to your arrival in Cancún, visit the Convention Bureau's website, **www.cancun.info**.

Pick up copies of the free monthly booklet, *Cancún Tips* (www.cancuntips.com.mx), and a seasonal tabloid of the same name.

More information about Mexico is available on the official site of Mexico's Tourism Promotion Board, **www.visitmexico.com**.

3 Entry Requirements & Customs

ENTRY REQUIREMENTS
PASSPORTS

All travelers to Mexico are required to present **photo identification** and **proof of citizenship,** such as a valid passport, naturalization papers, or an original birth certificate with a raised seal, along with a driver's license or official ID, such as a state or military issued ID. Driver's licenses and permits, voter registration cards, affidavits, and similar documents are not sufficient to prove citizenship for readmission into the United States. If the last name on the birth certificate is different from your current name, bring a photo identification card *and* legal proof of the name change, such as the original marriage license or certificate. *Note:* Photocopies are *not* acceptable.

Effective January 23, 2007, all U.S. citizens traveling by **air** to Mexico are required to have a valid passport to enter or reenter the United States. As early as January 1, 2008, U.S. citizens traveling between the United States and Mexico by **land** or **sea** may also be required to present a valid U.S. passport or other documents as determined by the Department of Homeland Security.

Safeguard your passport in an inconspicuous, inaccessible place like a money belt, and keep a copy of the critical pages with your passport number in a separate place. If you lose your passport, visit the nearest consulate of your native country as soon as possible for a replacement.

For information on how to get a passport, go to "Passports" in the "Fast Facts" section of this chapter—the websites listed provide downloadable passport applications as well as the current fees for processing passport applications. For an up-to-date, country-by-country listing of passport requirements around the world, go to the "Foreign Entry Requirement" Web page of the U.S. State Department at **http://travel.state.gov**.

ONCE YOU'RE IN MEXICO

You must carry a **Mexican Tourist Permit (FMT),** the equivalent of a tourist visa, which Mexican border officials issue, free of charge, after accepting your proof of citizenship (via your passport). Airlines generally provide the necessary forms aboard your flight to Mexico. The FMT is more important than a passport in Mexico, so guard it carefully. If you lose it, you may not be permitted to leave the

---

Tips Passport Savvy

Allow plenty of time before your trip to apply for a passport; processing normally takes 3 weeks but can take longer during busy periods (especially spring). And keep in mind that if you need a passport in a hurry, you'll pay a higher processing fee. When traveling, safeguard your passport in an inconspicuous, inaccessible place like a money belt and keep a copy of the critical pages with your passport number in a separate place. If you lose your passport, visit the nearest consulate or embassy of your native country as soon as possible for a replacement.

---

country until you can replace it—a bureaucratic hassle that can take anywhere from a few hours to a week.

The FMT can be issued for up to 180 days. Sometimes officials don't ask but just stamp a time limit, so be sure to say "6 months," or at least twice as long as you intend to stay. If you decide to extend your stay, you may request that additional time be added to your FMT from an official immigration office in Mexico.

Note: Children under age 18 who are traveling without parents or with only one parent must have a notarized letter from the absent parent(s) authorizing the travel. Mexican law requires that any non-Mexican under the age of 18 departing Mexico must carry notarized written permission from any parent or guardian not traveling with the child. This permission must include the name of the parent, the name of the child, the name of anyone traveling with the child, and the notarized signature(s) of the absent parent(s). The child must carry the original letter—not a copy—as well as proof of the parent/child relationship (usually a birth certificate or court document)—and an original custody decree, if applicable.

4 When to Go

SEASONS

High season in the Yucatán begins around December 20 and continues to Easter. This is the best time for calm, warm weather; snorkeling, diving, and fishing (the calmer weather means clearer and more predictable seas); and for visiting the ruins that dot the interior of the peninsula. Book well in advance if you plan to be in Cancún around the holidays.

Low season begins the day after Easter and continues to mid-December; during low season, prices may drop 20% to 50%. In Cancún and along the Riviera Maya, demand by European visitors is creating a summer high season, with hotel rates approaching those charged in the winter months.

Generally speaking, Mexico's **dry season** runs from November to April, with the **rainy season** stretching from May to October. It isn't a problem if you're staying close to the beaches, but for those bent on road-tripping to Chichén Itzá, Uxmal, or other sites, temperatures and humidity in the interior can be downright stifling from May to July. Later in the rainy season, the frequency of **tropical storms** and **hurricanes** increases; such storms, of course, can put a crimp in your vacation. But they can lower temperatures, making climbing ruins a real joy, accompanied by cool air and a slight wind.

November is especially ideal for Yucatán travels. Cancún, Cozumel, and Isla Mujeres also have a rainy season from November to January, when northern storms hit. This usually means diving visibility is diminished—and conditions may prevent boats from even going out.

Villahermosa is sultry and humid all the time. San Cristóbal de las Casas, at an elevation of 2,152m (7,059 ft.), is much cooler than the lowlands and is downright cold in winter.

5 Getting There & Getting Around

GETTING THERE

If this is not your first trip to Cancún, you'll notice that the airport's facilities and services continue to expand. **AeroMéxico** (© **800/ 237-6639** in the U.S., or 01/800-021-4000 in Mexico; www.aero mexico.com) offers connecting service to Cancún through Mexico City. **Mexicana** (© **800/531-7921** in the U.S., 01/800-502-2000 in Mexico, or 998/881-9090; www.mexicana.com.mx) offers connecting flights to Cancún through Miami or Mexico City. In addition to these carriers, many **charter** companies—such as Apple Vacations and Funjet—travel to Cancún; these package tours make up as much as 60% of arrivals by U.S. visitors (see "Packages for the Independent Traveler," later in this chapter).

Regional carrier **Click Mexicana,** a Mexicana affiliate (© **01- 800/112-5425** toll-free in Mexico; www.click.com.mx) flies from Cozumel, Havana, Mexico City, Mérida, Chetumal, and other points within Mexico. You'll want to confirm departure times for flights to the U.S. **Aviacsa** (© **01-800/711-6733** toll-free in Mexico; www.aviacsa.com) and **InterJet** (© **01-800/01-12345** toll-free in Mexico; www.interjet.com.mx) are two other regional carriers that fly to Cancún from Mexico City.

Here are the U.S. numbers of major international carriers serving Cancún: **Alaska** (© 800/426-0333; www.alaskaair.com), **American** (© 800/433-7300; www.aa.com), **Continental** (© 800/231-0856; www.continental.com), **Delta** (© 800/221-1212; www.delta.com), **Northwest** (© 800/225-2525; www.nwa.com), and **US Airways** (© 800/428-4322; www.usairways.com).

Most major car-rental firms have outlets at the airport, so if you're renting a car, consider picking it up and dropping it off at the airport to save on airport-transportation costs. Another way to save money is to arrange for the rental before you leave home. If you wait until you arrive, the daily cost will be around $50 to $75 (£28–£41) for a

Chevrolet Atos. Major agencies include **Avis** (©️ 800/331-1212 in the U.S., or 998/886-0221; www.avis.com); **Budget** (©️ 800/527-0700 in the U.S., or 998/886-0417; fax 998/884-4812; www.budget.com); **Dollar** (©️ 800/800-3665 in the U.S., or 998/886-2300; www.dollar.com); **National** (©️ 800/227-7368 in the U.S., or 998/886-0153; www.nationalcar.com); and **Hertz** (©️ 800/654-3131 in the U.S. and Canada, or 998/884-1326; www.hertz.com). If you're looking for an exotic car rental (such as a Porsche or Mercedes convertible) and don't mind paying a small fortune for it, try **Platinum** (©️ 998/883-5555; www.platinumcarrental.com), with an office inside the JW Marriott hotel. The Zona Hotelera (Hotel Zone) lies 10km (6¼ miles)—a 20-minute drive—from the airport along wide, well-paved roads.

Rates for a **private taxi** from the airport are around $25 (£14) to downtown Cancún, or $28 to $40 (£15–£22) to the Hotel Zone, depending on your destination. *Colectivos* (vans) run from the airport into town. Buy tickets, which cost about $10 (£5.50), from the booth to the far right as you exit the airport terminal. There's **minibus** transportation ($9.50/£5.25) from the airport to the Puerto Juárez passenger ferry to Isla Mujeres, or you can hire a private taxi for about $40 (£22). There is no *colectivo* service returning to the airport from Ciudad Cancún or the Hotel Zone, so you'll have to take a taxi, but the rate will be much less than for the trip from the airport. (Only federally chartered taxis may take fares *from* the airport, but any taxi may bring passengers *to* the airport.) Ask at your hotel what the fare should be, but expect to pay about half what you paid from the airport to your hotel.

BY CAR

From Mérida or Campeche, take **Highway 180** east to Cancún. This is mostly a winding, two-lane road that branches off into the express **toll road 180D** between Izamal and Nuevo Xcan. Nuevo Xcan is approximately 40km (25 miles) from Cancún. Mérida is about 80km (50 miles) away.

BY BUS

Cancún's **ADO bus terminal** (©️ **998/884-4352** or -4804) is in downtown Ciudad Cancún at the intersection of avenidas Tulum and Uxmal. All out-of-town buses arrive here. Buses run to Playa del Carmen, Tulum, Chichén Itzá, other nearby beach and archaeological zones, and other points within Mexico.

GETTING AROUND
BY TAXI

Taxi prices in Cancún are clearly set by zone, although keeping track of what's in which zone can take some doing. The minimum fare within the Hotel Zone is $6 per ride, making it one of the most expensive taxi areas in Mexico. In addition, taxis operating in the Hotel Zone feel perfectly justified in having a discriminatory pricing structure: Local residents pay about half of what tourists pay, and prices for guests at higher-priced hotels are about double those for budget hotel guests—these are all established by the taxi union. Rates should be posted outside your hotel; if you have a question, all drivers are required to have an official rate card in their taxis, though it's generally in Spanish.

Within the downtown area, the cost is about $1.50 (85p) per cab ride (not per person); within any other zone, it's $6 (£3.30). Traveling between two zones will also cost $6 (£3.30), and if you cross two zones, that'll cost $8 (£4.40). Settle on a price in advance, or check at your hotel. Trips to the airport from most zones cost $15 (£8.25). Taxis can also be rented for $18 (£9.90) per hour for travel around the city and Hotel Zone, but this rate can generally be negotiated down to about $15 (£8.25). If you want to hire a taxi to take you to Chichén Itzá or along the Riviera Maya, expect to pay about $30 (£17) per hour—many taxi drivers feel that they are also providing guide services.

BY BUS

Bus travel within Cancún continues to improve and is increasingly popular. In town, almost everything lies within walking distance. **Ruta 1** and **Ruta 2** (HOTELES) city buses travel frequently from the mainland to the beaches along Avenida Tulum (the main street) and all the way to Punta Nizuc at the far end of the Hotel Zone on Isla Cancún. **Ruta 8** buses go to Puerto Juárez/Punta Sam for ferries to Isla Mujeres. They stop on the east side of Avenida Tulum. All these city buses operate between 6am and 10pm daily. Beware of private buses along the same route; they charge far more than the public ones. Public buses have the fare painted on the front; at press time, the fare was 60¢ (Ᵽ33).

BY MOPED

Mopeds are a convenient but dangerous way to cruise around through the very congested traffic. Rentals start at $30 (£17) for a day, and a credit card voucher is required as security. You should receive a crash helmet (it's the law) and instructions on how to lock the wheels when you park. Read the fine print on the back of the rental agreement regarding liability for repairs or replacement in case of accident, theft, or vandalism.

6 Money & Costs

CURRENCY

The currency in Mexico is the Mexican **peso.** Paper currency comes in denominations of 20, 50, 100, 200, 500, and 1,000 pesos. Coins come in denominations of 1, 2, 5, 10, and 20 pesos, and 20 and 50 **centavos** (100 centavos = 1 peso). The current exchange rate for the U.S. dollar, and the one used in this book, is around 11 pesos; at that rate, an item that costs 11 pesos would be equivalent to US$1. The current exchange rate for the British pound is .55 to $1 U.S.

Getting **change** is a problem. Small-denomination bills and coins are hard to come by, so start collecting them early in your trip. Shopkeepers everywhere always seem to be out of change and small bills; that's doubly true in markets.

Many establishments that deal with tourists, especially in coastal resort areas, quote prices in dollars. To avoid confusion, they use the abbreviations "Dlls." for dollars and "M.N." (*moneda nacional,* or national currency) for pesos.

Don't forget to have enough pesos to carry you over a weekend or Mexican holiday, when banks are closed. In general, avoid carrying the U.S. $100 bill; it's the bill most commonly counterfeited in Mexico and therefore the most difficult to exchange, especially in smaller towns. Because small bills and coins in pesos are hard to come by in Mexico, the $1 bill is very useful for tipping. A tip of U.S. coins cannot be exchanged into Mexican currency and is of no value to the service provider.

The bottom line on exchanging money: Ask first, and then shop around. Banks generally pay the top rates. Exchange houses *(casas de cambio),* however, are generally more convenient than banks because they have more locations and longer hours; the rate of exchange may

---

Money Matters

The **universal currency sign ($)** is used to indicate pesos in Mexico. The use of the symbol in this book, however, denotes U.S. currency.

Tips A Few Words about Prices

The peso's value continues to fluctuate—at press time, it was roughly 11 pesos to the dollar. Prices in this book (which are always given in U.S. dollars and British pounds) have been converted to U.S. dollars at 11 pesos to the dollar. Most hotels in Mexico—with the exception of places that receive little foreign tourism—quote prices in U.S. dollars. Thus, currency fluctuations are unlikely to affect the prices most hotels charge.

Mexico has a **value-added tax** of 15% (*Impuesto de Valor Agregado,* or IVA; pronounced "ee-vah") on most everything, including restaurant meals, bus tickets, and souvenirs. (Exceptions are Cancún, Cozumel, and Los Cabos, where the IVA is 10%; as ports of entry, they receive a break on taxes.) Hotels charge the usual 15% IVA, plus a locally administered bed tax of 2% (in most areas), for a total of 17%. In Cancún, Los Cabos, and Cozumel, hotels charge the 10% IVA plus 2% room tax. The prices quoted by hotels and restaurants do not necessarily include IVA. You may find that upper-end properties (three or more stars) quote prices without IVA included, while lower-priced hotels include IVA. Always ask to see a printed price sheet and always ask if the tax is included.

---

be the same as at a bank or slightly lower. Before leaving a bank or exchange-house window, count your change in front of the teller.

Large airports have currency-exchange counters that often stay open whenever flights are operating. Though convenient, they generally do not offer the most favorable rates.

A hotel's exchange desk commonly pays less favorable rates than banks; however, when the currency is in a state of flux, higher-priced hotels are known to pay higher rates than banks, in an effort to attract dollars. *Note:* In almost all cases, you receive a better rate by changing money first, then paying.

BANKS & ATMs

Banks in Mexico tend to be open weekdays from 9am until 5pm, and often for at least a half-day on Saturday. In larger resorts and cities such as Cancún, they can generally accommodate the exchange of dollars anytime during business hours. During times when the currency is in flux, a particular bank may not exchange dollars, so check before standing in line. Some, but not all, banks charge a service fee of about 1% to exchange traveler's checks. However, you can pay for most purchases directly with traveler's checks at the establishment's stated exchange rate. Don't even bother with personal checks drawn on a U.S. bank—the bank will wait for your check to clear, which can take weeks, before giving you your money.

Travelers to Cancún can easily withdraw money from **ATMs,** and the use of ATMs is perfectly safe—just use the same precautions you would at any ATM. Universal bankcards (such as the Cirrus and PLUS systems) can be used. This is a convenient way to withdraw money and avoid carrying too much with you at any time. The exchange rate is generally more favorable than that at a currency house. Most machines offer Spanish/English menus and dispense pesos, but some offer the option of withdrawing dollars. Be sure to check the daily withdrawal limit before you depart.

For **Cirrus** locations abroad, check ℂ **800/424-7787** or **www.mastercard.com**. For **PLUS** outlets abroad, check ℂ **800/843-7587** or **www.visa.com.** Before you leave home, check your daily withdrawal limit, and make sure that your personal identification number (PIN) works in international destinations. Also keep in mind that many banks impose a fee every time a card is used at a different bank's ATM, and that fee can be higher for international transactions (up to $5 or more) than for domestic ones. To compare banks' ATM fees within the U.S., use **www.bankrate.com**. For international withdrawal fees, ask your bank.

You can also get cash advances on your credit card at an ATM. Keep in mind that credit card companies try to protect themselves from theft by limiting the funds someone can withdraw outside their home country, so call your credit card company before you leave home. And keep in mind that you'll pay interest from the moment of your withdrawal, even if you pay your monthly bills on time.

CREDIT CARDS

Visa, MasterCard, and American Express are the most accepted cards in the Yucatán, as in the rest of Mexico. You'll be able to charge most hotel, restaurant, and store purchases, as well as almost all airline tickets, on your credit card. Pemex gas stations began to accept credit card purchases for gasoline in 2006, though this option may not be available everywhere and is usually not offered at night. You can get cash advances of several hundred dollars on your card, but there may be a wait of 20 minutes to 2 hours.

Charges will be made in pesos, then converted into dollars by the bank issuing the credit card. Generally you receive the favorable bank rate when paying by credit card. However, be aware that some establishments in Mexico add a 5%-to-7% surcharge when you pay with a credit card. This is especially true when using American Express. Many times, advertised discounts will not apply if you pay with a credit card.

TRAVELER'S CHECKS

You can buy traveler's checks at most banks. They are offered in denominations of $20, $50, $100, $500, and sometimes $1,000. Generally, you'll pay a service charge ranging from 1% to 4%.

The most popular traveler's checks are offered by **American Express** (© **800/807-6233,** or 800/221-7282 for card holders—this number accepts collect calls, offers service in several foreign languages, and exempts Amex gold and platinum cardholders from the 1% fee); **Visa** (© **800/732-1322**)—AAA members can obtain Visa checks for a $9.95 fee (for checks up to $1,500) at most AAA offices or by calling © **866/339-3378**; and **MasterCard** (© **800/223-9920**).

Be sure to keep a record of the traveler's checks serial numbers separate from your checks in the event that they are stolen or lost. You'll get a refund faster if you know the numbers.

American Express, Thomas Cook, Visa, and **MasterCard** offer **foreign currency traveler's checks**, useful if you're traveling to one country or to the euro zone; they're accepted at locations where dollar checks may not be.

Another option is the new prepaid traveler's check cards, reloadable cards that work much like debit cards but aren't linked to your checking account. The **American Express Travelers Cheque Card,** for example, requires a minimum deposit, sets a maximum balance, and has a one-time issuance fee of $14.95. You can withdraw money from an ATM (for a fee of $2.50 per transaction, not including bank fees), and the funds can be purchased in dollars, euros, or pounds. If you lose the card, your available funds will be refunded within 24 hours.

7 Travel Insurance

The cost of travel insurance varies widely, depending on the destination, the cost and length of your trip, your age and health, and the type of trip you're taking, but expect to pay between 5% and 8% of the vacation itself. You can get estimates from various providers through **InsureMyTrip.com**. Enter your trip cost and dates, your age, and other information, for prices from more than a dozen companies.

U.K. citizens and their families who make more than one trip abroad per year may find an annual travel insurance policy works out cheaper. Check **www.moneysupermarket.com**, which compares prices across a wide range of providers for single- and multi-trip policies.

Most big travel agents offer their own insurance and will probably try to sell you their package when you book a holiday. Think before you sign. **Britain's Consumers' Association** recommends that you insist on seeing the policy and reading the fine print before buying travel insurance. **The Association of British Insurers** (© 020/7600-3333; www.abi.org.uk) gives advice by phone and publishes *Holiday Insurance,* a free guide to policy provisions and prices. You might also shop around for better deals: Try **Columbus Direct** (© **0870/033-9988;** www.columbusdirect.net).

TRIP-CANCELLATION INSURANCE

Trip-cancellation insurance will help retrieve your money if you have to back out of a trip or depart early, or if your travel supplier goes bankrupt. Trip cancellation traditionally covers such events as sickness, natural disasters, and State Department advisories. The latest news in trip-cancellation insurance is the availability of **expanded hurricane coverage** and the **"any-reason"** cancellation coverage—which costs more but covers cancellations made for any reason. You won't get back 100% of your prepaid trip cost, but you'll be refunded a substantial portion. **TravelSafe** (© **888/885-7233;** www.travel safe.com) offers both types of coverage. Expedia also offers any-reason cancellation coverage for its air-hotel packages.

For details, contact one of the following recommended insurers: **Access America** (© 866/807-3982; www.accessamerica.com); **Travel Guard International** (© 800/826-4919; www.travelguard.com); **Travel Insured International** (© 800/243-3174; www.travelinsured. com); and **Travelex Insurance Services** (© 888/457-4602; www. travelex-insurance.com).

MEDICAL INSURANCE

For travel overseas, most U.S. health plans (including Medicare and Medicaid) do not provide coverage, and the ones that do often require you to pay for services upfront and reimburse you only after you return home.

As a safety net, you may want to buy travel medical insurance, particularly if you're traveling to a remote or high-risk area where emergency evacuation might be necessary. If you require additional medical insurance, try **MEDEX Assistance** (© 410/453-6300; www.medexassist.com) or **Travel Assistance International** (© 800/ 821-2828; www.travelassistance.com; for general information on services, call the company's **Worldwide Assistance Services, Inc.,** at © 800/777-8710).

Canadians should check with their provincial health plan offices or call **Health Canada** (© 866/225-0709; www.hc-sc.gc.ca) to find out the extent of their coverage and what documentation and receipts they must take home in case they are treated overseas.

LOST-LUGGAGE INSURANCE

On flights within the U.S., checked baggage is covered up to $3,000 per ticketed passenger. On round-trip international flights originating in the U.S, liability limits are about $1,400 per passenger. If you plan to check items more valuable than what's covered by the standard liability, see if your homeowner's policy covers your valuables, get baggage insurance as part of your comprehensive travel-insurance package, or buy Travel Guard's "BagTrak" product.

If your luggage is lost, immediately file a lost-luggage claim at the airport, detailing the luggage contents. Most airlines require that you report delayed, damaged, or lost baggage within 4 hours of arrival. The airlines are required to deliver luggage, once found, directly to your house or destination free of charge.

8 Health

STAYING HEALTHY
GENERAL AVAILABILITY OF HEALTHCARE

In most of the Yucatán's resort destinations, healthcare meeting U.S. standards is now available. Mexico's major cities are also known for their quality healthcare, although the facilities available may be sparser, and the equipment may be older than what is available at home. Prescription medicine is broadly available at Mexico pharmacies; however be aware that you may have to have a copy of your prescription or obtain a prescription from a local doctor.

Contact the **International Association for Medical Assistance to Travelers** (IAMAT; © 716/754-4883, or 416/652-0137 in Canada; www.iamat.org) for tips on travel and health concerns in the countries you're visiting, and lists of local, English-speaking doctors. The U.S. **Centers for Disease Control and Prevention** (© 800/311-3435; www.cdc.gov) provides up-to-date information on health hazards by region or country and offers tips on food safety. The website **www.tripprep.com**, sponsored by a consortium

---

Tips Over-the-Counter Drugs in Mexico

Antibiotics and other drugs that you'd need a prescription to buy in the States are often available over-the-counter in Mexican pharmacies. Mexican pharmacies also carry a limited selection of common over-the-counter cold, sinus, and allergy remedies.

---

of travel medicine practitioners, may also offer helpful advice on traveling abroad. You can find listings of reliable clinics overseas at the **International Society of Travel Medicine** (www.istm.org).

COMMON AILMENTS

HIGH-ALTITUDE HAZARDS   Travelers to certain regions of Mexico occasionally experience **elevation sickness,** which results from the relative lack of oxygen and the decrease in barometric pressure that characterizes high elevations (more than 1,515m/4,969 ft.). Symptoms include shortness of breath, fatigue, headache, insomnia, and even nausea. Mexico City is at 2,121m (6,957 ft.) above sea level, as are a number of other central and southern cities, such as San Cristóbal de las Casas (even higher than Mexico City). At high elevations, it takes about 10 days to acquire the extra red blood corpuscles you need to adjust to the scarcity of oxygen. To help your body acclimate, drink plenty of fluids, avoid alcoholic beverages, and don't overexert yourself during the first few days. If you have heart or lung problems, talk to your doctor before going above 2,424m (7,951 ft.).

BUGS, BITES & OTHER WILDLIFE CONCERNS   **Mosquitoes** and **gnats** are prevalent along the coast and in the Yucatán lowlands. Insect repellent *(repelente contra insectos)* is a must. If you'll be in these areas and are prone to bites, bring along a repellent that contains the active ingredient DEET. Avon's Skin So Soft also works extremely well. Another good remedy to keep the mosquitoes away is to mix citronella essential oil with basil, clove, and lavender essential oils. If you're sensitive to bites, pick up some antihistamine cream from a drugstore at home.

Most readers won't ever see an *alacrán* (scorpion). But if one stings you, go immediately to a hospital or a doctor. The one lethal scorpion found in some parts of Mexico is the *Centruroides*, part of the Buthidea family, characterized by a thin body, thick tale, and triangular-shaped sternum. Most deaths from these scorpions result within 24 hours of the sting as a result of respiratory or cardiovascular failure, with children and seniors most at risk. Scorpions are not aggressive (they don't hunt for prey), but they may sting if touched, especially in their hiding places. In Mexico you can buy scorpion toxin antidote at any drugstore. It is an injection and it costs around $25. This is a good idea if you plan to camp in a remote area where medical assistance can be several hours away.

MORE SERIOUS DISEASES   You shouldn't be overly concerned about tropical diseases if you stay on the normal tourist routes and don't eat street food. However, both dengue fever and cholera have appeared in Mexico in recent years. Talk to your doctor or to a medical specialist in tropical diseases about precautions you should take. You can also get medical bulletins from the U.S. State Department and the Centers for Disease Control and Prevention (see "Visitor Information," earlier in this chapter). You can protect yourself by taking some simple precautions: Watch what you eat and drink; don't swim in stagnant water (ponds, slow-moving rivers, or wells); and avoid mosquito bites by covering up, using repellent, and sleeping under netting. The most dangerous areas seem to be on Mexico's west coast, away from the big resorts.

WHAT TO DO IF YOU GET SICK AWAY FROM HOME

Any foreign consulate can provide a list of area doctors who speak English. If you get sick, consider asking your hotel concierge to recommend a local doctor—even his or her own. You can also try the emergency room at a local hospital. Many hospitals also have walk-in clinics for emergency cases that are not life-threatening; you may not get immediate attention, but you won't pay the high price of an emergency room visit. We list hospitals and emergency numbers under "Fast Facts" in chapter 4.

If you suffer from a chronic illness, consult your doctor before you depart. For conditions like epilepsy, diabetes, or heart problems, wear a **MedicAlert Identification Tag** (© **888/633-4298;** www. medicalert.org), which will immediately alert doctors to your condition and give them access to your records through MedicAlert's 24-hour hot line.

Pack **prescription medications** in your carry-on luggage, and carry them in their original containers, with pharmacy labels—otherwise they won't make it through airport security. Also bring along copies of your prescriptions in case you lose your pills or run out.

Don't forget an extra pair of contact lenses or prescription glasses. Carry the generic name of prescription medicines, in case a local pharmacist is unfamiliar with the brand name.

EMERGENCY EVACUATION   In extreme medical emergencies, a service from the United States will fly people to American hospitals. **Global Life Flights** (© **800/831-9307,** or 01-800/305-9400 in Mexico; www.globallifeflight.com) is a 24-hour air ambulance.

9 Safety

CRIME

Crime in Mexico, especially in Mexico City, in selected cities along the U.S. border, and in some states affected by drug violence, has received attention in the North American press over the past several years. Many feel this unfairly exaggerates the real dangers, but it should be noted that crime rates, including taxi robberies, kidnappings, and highway carjackings, have risen in recent years. The most severe problems have been concentrated in Mexico City, where even longtime foreign residents will attest to the overall lack of security. Violent crime has also continued at high levels in Tijuana, Ciudad Juarez, Nuevo Laredo, Acapulco, and the state of Sinaloa. The U.S. Department of State recommends caution in traveling to the southern states of Oaxaca, Chiapas, and Guerrero due to sporadic incidents of politically motivated violence there. Check the U.S. State Department Consular Information Sheet (and any applicable travel advisories) for Mexico before you travel to any notable "hot spots."

Precautions are necessary, but travelers should be realistic. Common sense is essential. You can generally trust people whom you approach for help or directions—but be wary of anyone who approaches you offering the same. The more insistent the person is, the more cautious you should be. The crime rate is, on the whole, much lower in Mexico than in many parts of the United States, and the nature of crimes in general is less violent.

Travelers should exercise caution in traveling Mexico's highways, avoiding travel at night, and using *cuota (*toll) roads rather than the less secure *libre* (free) roads whenever possible. It is also advised that you should not hike alone in backcountry areas, nor walk alone on scarcely frequented beaches, ruins, or trails.

BRIBES & SCAMS

As is the case around the world, there are the occasional bribes and scams in Mexico, targeted at people believed to be naive—such as

Tips Treating & Avoiding Digestive Trouble

It's called "travelers' diarrhea" or *turista*, the Spanish word for "tourist": persistent diarrhea, often accompanied by fever, nausea, and vomiting, that used to attack many travelers to Mexico. (Some in the U.S. call this "Montezuma's revenge," but you won't hear it called that in Mexico.) Widespread improvements in infrastructure, sanitation, and education have greatly diminished this ailment, especially in well-developed resort areas. Most travelers make a habit of drinking only bottled water, which also helps to protect against unfamiliar bacteria. In resort areas, and generally throughout Mexico, only purified ice is used. If you do come down with this ailment, nothing beats Pepto Bismol, readily available in Mexico. Imodium is also available in Mexico and is used by many travelers for a quick fix. A good high-potency (or "therapeutic") vitamin supplement and even extra vitamin C can help; yogurt is good for healthy digestion.

Since dehydration can quickly become life-threatening, the Public Health Service advises that you be careful to replace fluids and electrolytes (potassium, sodium, and the like) during a bout of diarrhea. Drink Pedialyte, a rehydration solution available at most Mexican pharmacies, or natural fruit juice, such as guava or apple (stay away from orange juice, which has laxative properties), with a pinch of salt added.

How to prevent it: The U.S. Public Health Service recommends the following measures for preventing travelers' diarrhea: **Drink only purified water** (boiled water, canned or bottled beverages, beer, or wine). **Choose food carefully.** In general, avoid salads (except in first-class restaurants), uncooked vegetables, undercooked protein, and unpasteurized milk or milk products, including cheese. Avoid eating food prepared by street vendors. Choose food that is freshly cooked and still hot. In addition, something as simple as **clean hands** can go a long way toward preventing *turista*.

the telltale tourist. For years, Mexico was known as a place where bribes—called *mordidas* (bites)—were expected; however, the country is rapidly changing. Frequently, offering a bribe today, especially to a police officer, is considered an insult, and it can land you in deeper trouble.

If you believe a **bribe** is being requested, here are a few tips on dealing with the situation. Even if you speak Spanish, don't utter a word of it to Mexican officials. That way you'll appear innocent while understanding every word.

When you are crossing the border, should the person who inspects your car ask for a tip, you can ignore this request—but understand that the official may suddenly decide that a complete search of your belongings is in order. If faced with a situation where you feel you're being asked for a *propina* (literally, "tip"; colloquially, "bribe"), how much should you offer? Usually $3 to $5 or the equivalent in pesos will do the trick. Many tourists have the impression that everything works better in Mexico if you "tip"; however, in reality, this only perpetuates the *mordida* attitude. If you are pleased with a service, feel free to tip, but you shouldn't tip simply to attempt to get away with something illegal or inappropriate, whether it is crossing the border without having your car inspected or not getting a ticket that's deserved.

Whatever you do, **avoid impoliteness;** under no circumstances should you insult a Latin American official. Extreme politeness, even in the face of adversity, rules Mexico. In Mexico, *gringos* have a reputation for being loud and demanding. By adopting the local custom of excessive courtesy, you'll have greater success in negotiations of any kind. Stand your ground, but do it politely.

As you travel in Mexico, you may encounter several types of **scams,** which are typical throughout the world. One involves some kind of a **distraction** or feigned commotion. While your attention is diverted, a pickpocket makes a grab for your wallet. In another common scam, an **unaccompanied child** pretends to be lost and frightened and takes your hand for safety. Meanwhile the child or an accomplice plunders your pockets. A third involves **confusing currency.** A shoeshine boy, street musician, guide, or other individual might offer you a service for a price that seems reasonable—in pesos. When it comes time to pay, he or she tells you the price is in dollars, not pesos. Be very clear on the price and currency when services are involved.

10 Specialized Travel Resources

TRAVELERS WITH DISABILITIES

Mexico may seem like one giant obstacle course to travelers in wheelchairs or on crutches. At airports, you may encounter steep stairs before finding a well-hidden elevator or escalator—if one exists. Airlines will often arrange wheelchair assistance to the baggage area. Porters are generally available to help with luggage at airports and large bus stations, once you've cleared baggage claim.

Mexican airports are upgrading their services, but it is not uncommon to board from a remote position, meaning you either descend stairs to a bus that ferries you to the plane, which you board by climbing stairs, or you walk across the tarmac to your plane and ascend the stairs. Deplaning presents the same problem in reverse.

Escalators (and there aren't many in the country) are often out of order. Stairs without handrails abound. Few restrooms are equipped for travelers with disabilities; when one is available, access to it may be through a narrow passage that won't accommodate a wheelchair or a person on crutches. Many deluxe hotels (the most expensive) now have rooms with bathrooms for people with disabilities. Those traveling on a budget should stick with one-story hotels or hotels with elevators. Even so, there will probably still be obstacles somewhere. Generally speaking, no matter where you are, someone will lend a hand, although you may have to ask for it.

Most disabilities shouldn't stop anyone from traveling. There are more options and resources out there than ever before.

Organizations that offer assistance to disabled travelers include **MossRehab** (© **1-800-CALLMOSS** or 215/456-9900; www.moss resourcenet.org), which provides a library of accessible-travel resources online; the **American Foundation for the Blind (AFB; © 800/232-5463;** www.afb.org), a referral resource for the blind or visually impaired that includes information on traveling with Seeing Eye dogs; and **SATH** (Society for Accessible Travel & Hospitality; © **800/513-1126;** www.sath.org; annual membership fees: $49 adults, $29 seniors and students), which offers a wealth of travel resources for all types of disabilities and informed recommendations on destinations, access guides, travel agents, tour operators, vehicle rentals, and companion services. **AirAmbulanceCard.com** is now partnered with SATH and allows you to preselect top-notch hospitals in case of an emergency for $195 a year ($295 per family), among other benefits.

For more information, check out the quarterly magazine *Emerging Horizons* (www.emerginghorizons.com; $17 per year, $22 outside the U.S.); and *Open World* magazine, published by SATH (see above; subscription: $13 per year, $21 outside the U.S.).

GAY & LESBIAN TRAVELERS

Mexico is a conservative country, with deeply rooted Catholic religious traditions. Public displays of same-sex affection are still rare in most parts of the country, especially outside of urban or resort areas. Women in Mexico frequently walk hand in hand, but anything more would cross the boundary of acceptability. However, gay and lesbian travelers are generally treated with respect and should not experience any harassment, assuming they give the appropriate regard to local culture and customs.

The **International Gay and Lesbian Travel Association** (IGLTA; ℭ **800/448-8550** or 954/776-2626; www.iglta.org) is the trade association for the gay and lesbian travel industry, and offers an online directory of gay- and lesbian-friendly travel businesses; go to their website and click on "Members."

Many agencies offer tours and travel itineraries specifically for gay and lesbian travelers. **Above and Beyond Tours** (ℭ **800/397-2681**; www.abovebeyondtours.com) is the exclusive gay and lesbian tour operator for United Airlines. **Now, Voyager** (ℭ **800/255-6951**; www.nowvoyager.com) is a well-known San Francisco–based, gay-owned and -operated travel service. **Olivia Cruises & Resorts** (ℭ **800/631-6277**; www.olivia.com) charters entire resorts and ships for exclusive lesbian vacations and offers smaller group experiences for both gay and lesbian travelers.

Gay.com Travel (ℭ **415/644-8044**; www.gay.com/travel or www.outandabout.com), is an excellent online successor to the popular *Out & About* print magazine. It provides regularly updated information about gay-owned, gay-oriented, and gay-friendly lodging, dining, sightseeing, nightlife, and shopping establishments in every important destination worldwide. It also offers trip-planning information for gay and lesbian travelers for more than 50 destinations, along various themes, ranging from "Sex & Travel" to "Vacations for Couples."

The following travel guides are available at many bookstores, or you can order them from any online bookseller: *Frommer's Gay & Lesbian Europe* (www.frommers.com), an excellent travel resource to the top European cities and resorts; *Spartacus International*

Gay Guide (Bruno Gmünder Verlag; www.spartacusworld.com/gay guide); and *Odysseus: The International Gay Travel Planner* (Odysseus Enterprises Ltd.), both good, annual, English-language guidebooks focused on gay men; and the *Damron* guides (www. damron.com), with separate, annual books for gay men and lesbians.

SENIOR TRAVEL

Mexico is a popular country for retirees. For decades, North Americans have been living indefinitely in Mexico by returning to the border and re-crossing with a new tourist permit every 6 months. Mexican immigration officials have caught on, and now limit the maximum time in the country to 6 months within any year. This is to encourage even partial residents to acquire proper documentation.

Some of the most popular places for long-term stays are Guadalajara, Lake Chapala, Ajijic, and Puerto Vallarta, all in the state of Jalisco; San Miguel de Allende and Guanajuato in Guanajuato state; Cuernavaca in Morelos; and Alamos in Sinaloa. The Caribbean coast of the Yucatán is becoming an increasingly popular place to invest and retire as well.

AIM, Apdo. Postal 31–70, 45050 Guadalajara, Jal., is a well-written, informative newsletter for prospective retirees. Issues have evaluated retirement in Aguascalientes, Puebla, San Cristóbal de las Casas, Puerto Angel, Puerto Escondido and Huatulco, Oaxaca, Taxco, Tepic, Manzanillo, Melaque, and Barra de Navidad. Subscriptions are $18 to the United States and $25 to Canada. Back issues are three for $5.

Sanborn Tours, 2015 S. 10th St., Post Office Drawer 519, McAllen, TX 78505-0519 (℃ **800/454-5768;** www.sanborns.com) offers a "Retire in Mexico" orientation tour.

Mention the fact that you're a senior when you make your travel reservations. Although all the major U.S. airlines have canceled their senior discount and coupon book programs, many hotels still offer lower rates for seniors. In most cities, people over the age of 60 qualify for reduced admission to theaters, museums, and other attractions, and discounted fares on public transportation.

Members of **AARP** (formerly known as the American Association of Retired Persons), 601 E St. NW, Washington, DC 20049 (℃ **888/ 687-2277;** www.aarp.org), get discounts on hotels, airfares, and car rentals. AARP offers members a wide range of benefits, including *AARP: The Magazine* and a monthly newsletter. Anyone over 50 can join.

Many reliable agencies and organizations target the 50-plus market. **Elderhostel** (𝒞 **877/426-8056;** www.elderhostel.org) arranges study programs for those aged 55 and over (and a spouse or companion of any age) in the U.S. and in more than 80 countries around the world. Most courses last 5 to 7 days in the U.S. (2–4 weeks abroad), and many include airfare, accommodations in university dormitories or modest inns, meals, and tuition. **ElderTreks** (𝒞 **800/741-7956;** www.eldertreks.com) offers small-group tours to off-the-beaten-path or adventure-travel locations, restricted to travelers 50 and older. Recommended publications offering travel resources and discounts for seniors include the quarterly magazine *Travel 50 & Beyond* (www.travel50andbeyond.com); *Travel Unlimited: Uncommon Adventures for the Mature Traveler* (Avalon); *101 Tips for Mature Travelers,* available from Grand Circle Travel (𝒞 **800/221-2610** or 617/350-7500; www.gct.com); and *Unbelievably Good Deals and Great Adventures That You Absolutely Can't Get Unless You're Over 50* (McGraw-Hill), by Joann Rattner Heilman.

FAMILY TRAVEL

Children are considered the national treasure of Mexico, and Mexicans will warmly welcome and cater to your children. Many parents were reluctant to bring young children into Mexico in the past, primarily due to health concerns, but I can't think of a better place to introduce children to the exciting adventure of exploring a different culture. Cancún is one of the best destinations. Hotels can often arrange for a babysitter.

Before leaving, ask your doctor which medications to take along. Disposable diapers cost about the same in Mexico but are of poorer quality. You can get Huggies Supreme and Pampers identical to the ones sold in the United States, but at a higher price. Many stores sell Gerber's baby foods. Dry cereals, powdered formulas, baby bottles, and purified water are easily available in midsize and large cities or resorts.

Cribs may present a problem; only the largest and most luxurious hotels provide them. However, rollaway beds are often available. Child seats or highchairs in restaurants are common.

Consider bringing your own car seat; they are not readily available for rent in Mexico.

Every country's regulations differ, but in general children traveling abroad should have plenty of documentation on hand, particularly if they're traveling with someone other than their own parents

Tips **Advice for Female Travelers**

Mexicans in general, and men in particular, are nosy about single travelers, especially women. If a taxi driver or anyone else with whom you don't want to become friendly asks about your marital status, family, and so forth, my advice is to make up a set of answers (regardless of the truth): "I'm married, traveling with friends, and I have three children." Saying you're single and traveling alone may send the wrong message. U.S. television—widely viewed now in Mexico—has given many Mexican men the image of American single women as being sexually promiscuous. Check out the award-winning website **Journeywoman** (www.journeywoman.com), a "real-life" women's travel information network; or the travel guide *Safety and Security for Women Who Travel* by Sheila Swan and Peter Laufer (Travelers' Tales, Inc.), offering common-sense tips on safe travel.

(in which case a notarized form letter from a parent is often required). For details on entry requirements for children traveling abroad, go to the U.S. State Department website (www.travel.state. gov); click on "International Travel," "Travel Brochures," and "Foreign Entry Requirements."

Throughout this book, the "Kids" icon distinguishes attractions, hotels, restaurants, and other destinations that are particularly attractive and accommodating to children and families.

Recommended family travel Internet sites include **Family Travel Forum** (www.familytravelforum.com), a comprehensive site that offers customized trip planning; **Family Travel Network** (www.familytravelnetwork.com), an award-winning site that offers travel features, deals, and tips; **Traveling Internationally with Your Kids** (www.travelwithyourkids.com), a comprehensive site offering sound advice for long-distance and international travel with children; and **Family Travel Files** (www.thefamilytravelfiles.com), which offers an online magazine and a directory of off-the-beaten-path tours and tour operators for families.

STUDENT TRAVEL

Because many Mexicans consider higher education more a luxury than a birthright, there is no formal network of student discounts and programs. Most Mexican students travel with their families rather than with other students, so student discount cards are not commonly recognized.

However, more hostels have entered the student travel scene. The **Mexican Youth Hostel Association,** or Asociación Mexicana de Albergues Juveniles (www.hostels.com./en/mx.html), offers a list of hostels in Tulum, Cancún, and Playa del Carmen, and other towns and cities outside the Yucatán.

If you're a student planning to travel outside the U.S., you'd be wise to arm yourself with an **International Student Identity Card (ISIC),** which offers substantial savings on rail passes, plane tickets, and entrance fees. It also provides you with basic health and life insurance and a 24-hour help line. The card is available from **STA Travel** (*(C)* **800/781-4040** in North America; www.sta.com or www.statravel.com), the biggest student travel agency in the world. If you're no longer a student but are still under 26, you can get an **International Youth Travel Card (IYTC)** for the same price from the same people, which entitles you to some discounts (but not on museum admissions). **Travel CUTS** (*(C)* **800/667-2887** or 416/614-2887; www.travelcuts.com) offers similar services for both Canadians and U.S. residents. Irish students may prefer to turn to **USIT** (*(C)* **01/602-1600;** www.usitnow.ie), an Ireland-based specialist in student, youth, and independent travel.

11 Sustainable Tourism/Ecotourism

Each time you take a flight or drive a car CO_2 is released into the atmosphere. You can help neutralize this danger to our planet through "carbon offsetting"—paying someone to reduce your CO_2 emissions by the same amount you've added. Carbon offsets can be purchased in the U.S. from companies such as **Carbonfund.org** (www.carbonfund.org) and **TerraPass** (www.terrapass.org), and from **Climate Care** (www.climatecare.org) in the U.K.

Although one could argue that any vacation that includes an airplane flight can't be truly "green," you can go on holiday and still contribute positively to the environment. You can offset carbon emissions from your flight in other ways. Choose forward-looking companies that embrace responsible development practices, helping preserve destinations for the future by working alongside local people. An increasing number of sustainable tourism initiatives can help you plan a family trip and leave as small a "footprint" as possible on the places you visit.

Responsible Travel (www.responsibletravel.com) contains a great source of sustainable travel ideas run by a spokesperson for responsible tourism in the travel industry. **Sustainable Travel International** (www.sustainabletravelinternational.org) promotes responsible tourism practices and issues an annual Green Gear & Gift Guide.

You can find eco-friendly travel tips, statistics, and touring companies and associations—listed by destination under "Travel Choice"—at the TIES website, www.ecotourism.org. Also check out **Conservation International** (www.conservation.org)—which, with *National Geographic Traveler,* annually presents **World Legacy Awards** (www.wlaward.org) to those travel tour operators, businesses, organizations, and places that have made a significant contribution to sustainable tourism. **Ecotravel.com** is part online magazine and part ecodirectory that lets you search for touring companies in several categories (water-based, land-based, spiritually oriented, and so on).

In the U.K., **Tourism Concern** (www.tourismconcern.org.uk) works to reduce social and environmental problems connected to tourism and find ways of improving tourism so that local benefits are increased.

Tips It's Easy Being Green

We can all help conserve fuel and energy when we travel. Here are a few simple ways you can help preserve your favorite destinations:

- Whenever possible, choose nonstop flights; they generally require less fuel than those that must stop and take off again.
- If renting a car is necessary on your vacation, ask the rental agent for the most fuel-efficient car available. Not only will you use less gas, you'll save money at the tank.
- At hotels, request that your sheets and towels not be changed daily. You'll save water and energy by not washing them as often, and you'll prolong the life of the towels, too. (Many hotels already have programs like this in place.)
- Turn off the lights and air conditioner (or heater) when you leave your hotel room.

Frommers.com: The Complete Travel Resource

It should go without saying, but we highly recommend **Frommers.com**, voted Best Travel Site by *PC Magazine*. We think you'll find our expert advice and tips; independent reviews of hotels, restaurants, attractions, and preferred shopping and nightlife venues; vacation giveaways; and an online booking tool indispensable before, during, and after your travels. We publish the complete contents of more than 128 travel guides in our **Destinations** section covering nearly 3,600 places worldwide to help you plan your trip. Each weekday, we publish original articles reporting on **Deals and News** via our free **Frommers.com Newsletter** to help you save time and money and travel smarter. We're betting you'll find our new **Events** listings (http://events.frommers.com) an invaluable resource; it's an up-to-the-minute roster of what's happening in cities everywhere—including concerts, festivals, lectures and more. We've also added weekly **Podcasts, interactive maps,** and hundreds of new images across the site. Check out our **Travel Talk** area featuring **Message Boards** where you can join in conversations with thousands of fellow Frommer's travelers and post your trip report once you return.

The **Association of British Travel Agents (ABTA;** www.abta members.org/responsibletourism) acts as a focal point for the U.K. travel industry and is one of the leading groups spearheading responsible tourism.

The **Association of Independent Tour Operators (AITO;** www. aito.co.uk) is a group of interesting specialist operators leading the field in making holidays sustainable.

For information about the ethics of swimming with dolphins and other outdoor activities, visit the **Whale and Dolphin Conservation Society** (www.wdcs.org) and **Tread Lightly** (www.treadlightly.org).

For companies that specialize in ecotourism in Mexico, see "The Active Traveler," later in this chapter.

12 Staying Connected

TELEPHONES

To call Mexico:

1. Dial the international access code: 011 from the U.S.; 00 from the U.K., Ireland, or New Zealand; or 0011 from Australia.
2. Dial the country code: 52.
3. Dial the two- or three-digit area code, then the eight- or seven-digit number. For example, if you wanted to call the U.S. consular agent in Acapulco, the whole number would be 011-52-744-469-0556. If you wanted to dial the U.S. Embassy in Mexico City, the whole number would be 011-52-55-5080-2000.

To make international calls: To make international calls from Mexico, first dial 00, then the country code (U.S. or Canada 1, U.K. 44, Ireland 353, Australia 61, New Zealand 64). Next, dial the area code and number. For example, to call the British Embassy in Washington, you would dial 00-1-202-588-7800.

For directory assistance: Dial ℂ 040 if you're looking for a number inside Mexico. *Note:* Listings usually appear under the owner's name, not the name of the business, and your chances to find an English-speaking operator are slim to none.

For operator assistance: If you need operator assistance in making a call, dial **090** to make an international call, and **020** to call a number in Mexico.

Toll-free numbers: Numbers beginning with 800 within Mexico are toll-free, but calling a U.S. toll-free number from Mexico costs the same as an overseas call. To call an 800 number in the U.S., dial 001-880 and the last seven digits of the toll-free number. To call an 888 number in the U.S., dial 001-881 and the last seven digits of the toll-free number. For a number with an 887 prefix, dial 882; for 866, dial 883.

CELLPHONES

The three letters that define much of the world's wireless capabilities are **GSM** (Global System for Mobile Communications)—a big, seamless network that makes for easy cross-border cellphone use worldwide. In the U.S., T-Mobile, AT&T Wireless, and Cingular use this quasi-universal system; in Canada, Microcell and some Rogers customers are GSM; and all Europeans and most Australians use GSM. GSM phones function with a removable plastic SIM card, encoded with your phone number and account information. If your cellphone is on a GSM system, and you have a world-capable multiband phone such as many Sony Ericsson, Motorola, or Samsung models, you can make and receive calls across civilized areas around much of the globe. Just call your wireless operator and ask for "international roaming" to be activated on your account. Unfortunately, per-minute charges can be high.

Mexico doesn't offer many cellphone rental options yet. Rentals aren't common in either airports or with the national (monopoly) telephone company. One option in Cancún is a company called **Phone Rental** (℃ **55/5250-9996;** www.phonerental.com.mx; Av. Ejercito Nacional 505, Suite 603). This international cellphone service will deliver a cellphone to you in Cancún, Merida, Playa del Carmen, or Isla Mujeres. Clients can make arrangements via e-mail or phone. The first week of the phone rental is free, and clients pay only the costs of the calls.

North Americans can rent a phone before leaving home from **InTouch USA** (℃ **800/872-7626;** www.intouchglobal.com) or **RoadPost** (℃ **888/290-1606** or 905/272-5665; www.roadpost.com). InTouch will also, for free, advise you on whether your existing phone will work overseas; simply call ℃ **703/222-7161** between 9am and 4pm EST, or go to **http://intouchglobal.com/travel.htm**.

VOICE-OVER INERNET PROTOCOL (VOIP)

If you have web access while traveling, you might consider a broadband-based telephone service (in technical terms, **Voice-over Internet protocol,** or **VoIP**) such as Skype (www.skype.com) or Vonage (www.vonage.com), which allows you to make free international calls if you use their services from your laptop or in a cybercafe. The people you're calling must also use the service for it to work; check the sites for details.

INTERNET/E-MAIL
WITHOUT YOUR OWN COMPUTER

To find cybercafes in Cancún, check **www.cybercaptive.com** and **www.cybercafe.com**. Most major airports have **Internet kiosks** that provide basic Web access for a per-minute fee that's usually higher than cybercafe prices.

WITH YOUR OWN COMPUTER

More and more hotels, resorts, airports, cafes, and retailers are going **Wi-Fi** (wireless fidelity), becoming "hotspots" that offer free

Online Traveler's Toolbox

Veteran travelers usually carry some essential items to make their trips easier. Following is a selection of handy online tools to bookmark and use.

- **Airplane Food** (www.airlinemeals.net)
- **Airplane Seating** (www.seatguru.com and www.airline quality.com)
- **Foreign Languages for Travelers** (www.travlang.com)
- **Maps** (www.mapquest.com)
- **Subway Navigator** (www.subwaynavigator.com)
- **Time and Date** (www.timeanddate.com)
- **Travel Warnings** (http://travel.state.gov, www.fco.gov. uk/travel, www.voyage.gc.ca, or www.dfat.gov.au/consular/advice)
- **Universal Currency Converter** (www.xe.com/ucc)
- **Visa ATM Locator** (www.visa.com), **MasterCard ATM Locator** (www.mastercard.com)
- **Weather** (www.intellicast.com and www.weather.com)

high-speed Wi-Fi access or charge a small fee for usage. Most laptops sold today have built-in wireless capability. To find public Wi-Fi hotspots at your destination, go to **www.jiwire.com**; its Hotspot Finder holds the world's largest directory of public wireless hotspots.

For dial-up access, most business-class hotels throughout the world offer dataports for laptop modems, and a few thousand hotels in Europe now offer free high-speed Internet access.

Wherever you go, bring a **connection kit** of the right power and phone adapters, a spare phone cord, and a spare Ethernet network cable—or find out whether your hotel supplies them to guests. The electrical system in Mexico is 110 volts AC (60 cycles), as in the United States and Canada, and phone adapters are the same, as well.

THE BEST CANCUN WEBSITES

- www.cancun.com.mx
- www.gocancun.com
- www.cancun.com
- www.go2cancun.com
- www.cancun.info

13 Packages for the Independent Traveler

Package tours are simply a way to buy the airfare, accommodations, and other elements of your trip (such as car rentals, airport transfers, and sometimes even activities) at the same time and often at discounted prices.

One good source of package deals is the airlines themselves. Most major airlines offer air/land packages, including **American Airlines Vacations** (© 800/321-2121; www.aavacations.com), **Delta Vacations** (© 800/654-6559; www.deltavacations.com), **Continental Airlines Vacations** (© 800/301-3800; www.covacations.com), and **United Vacations** (© 888/854-3899; www.unitedvacations.com). Several big **online travel agencies**—Expedia, Travelocity, Orbitz, Site59, and Lastminute.com—also do a brisk business in packages.

Aeroméxico Vacations (© **800/245-8585;** www.aeromexico. com) offers year-round packages to almost every destination it serves, including Cancún and Cozumel. Aeroméxico has a large (more than 100) selection of resorts in these destinations and more, in a variety of price ranges. The best deals are from Houston, Dallas, San Diego, Los Angeles, Miami, and New York, in that order.

Mexico Travel Net (www.mexicotravelnet.com), also offers most of the well-known travel packages to Mexico beach resorts, plus offers last-minute specials.

From the East Coast: Liberty Travel (© **888/271-1584;** www. libertytravel.com), one of the biggest packagers in the Northeast, often runs a full-page ad in the Sunday papers, with frequent Mexico specials. You won't get much in the way of service, but you will get a good deal.

From the West: Suntrips (© **800/248-7471** for departures within 14 days; www.suntrips.com) is one of the largest West Coast packagers for Mexico, with departures from San Francisco and Denver; regular charters to Cancún and other Mexican locations; and a large selection of hotels.

From the Southwest: Town and Country (book through travel agents) packages regular deals to Cancún with America West from the airline's Phoenix and Las Vegas gateways.

Resort Packages: The biggest hotel chains and resorts also sell packages. To take advantage of these offers, contact your travel agent or call the hotels directly.

Travel packages are also listed in the travel section of your local Sunday newspaper. Or check ads in national travel magazines such

> **Tips   Questions to Ask Tour Operators**
>
> Before you invest in a package deal or an escorted tour:
>
> - Always ask about the **cancellation policy**. Can you get your money back? Is there a deposit required?
> - Ask about the **accommodations choices and prices** for each. Then look up the hotels' reviews in a Frommer's guide and check their rates online for your specific dates of travel. Also find out what types of rooms are offered.
> - Request a complete **schedule**. (Escorted tours only.)
> - Ask about the **size** and demographics of the group. (Escorted tours only.)
> - Discuss what is included in the **price**: transportation, meals, tips, airport transfers, and so on. (Escorted tours only.)
> - Finally, look for **hidden expenses**. Ask whether airport departure fees and taxes, for example, are included in the total cost—they rarely are.

as *Arthur Frommer's Budget Travel Magazine, Travel + Leisure, National Geographic Traveler,* and *Condé Nast Traveler.*

RECOMMENDED TOUR OPERATORS IN THE YUCATAN

- **Caribbean Coast Travel**
  (www.caribbeancoasttravel.com)
- **Espresso Maya Train**
  (www.railsnw.com)
- **Mayan Expeditions**
  (www.mayanexpeditions.com)
- **SS-Tours**
  (www.ss-tours.com/yucatan.html)
- **Yucatán Spiritual Mayan Tours**
  (www.iluminado-tours.com)

14 Special-Interest Trips

THE ACTIVE TRAVELER

GOLF   Golf courses are plentiful in Cancún and Playa del Carmen. Visitors can also enjoy **tennis, water-skiing, surfing, bicycling,** and

horseback riding. Snorkeling and **scuba diving** are excellent off the Yucatán's Caribbean coast; Cozumel is considered one of the top five dive spots in the world.

PARKS   Many of the national parks and nature reserves are understaffed or unstaffed. Reliable Mexican companies (such as **AMTAVE** members; see below) and many U.S.-based companies offer adventure trips.

OUTDOORS ORGANIZATIONS & TOUR OPERATORS

AMTAVE (Asociación Mexicana de Turismo de Aventura y Ecoturismo, A.C.) is an active association of eco- and adventure-tour operators. It publishes an annual catalog of participating firms and their offerings, all of which must meet certain criteria for security, quality, and training of the guides, as well as for sustainability of natural and cultural environments. For more information, contact AMTAVE (© **55/5688-3883;** www.amtave.org).

   The Archaeological Conservancy, 5301 Central Ave. NE, Suite 402, Albuquerque, NM 87108 (© **505/266-1540;** www.american archaeology.com/tour.html), presents one trip to Mexico per year led by an expert, usually an archaeologist. The trips change from year to year and space is limited; make reservations early.

   ATC Tours and Travel, Av. 16 de Septiembre 16, 29200 San Cristóbal de las Casas, Chi. (© **967/678-2550** or 967/678-2557; fax 967/678-3145; www.atctours.com), a Mexico-based tour operator with an excellent reputation, offers specialist-led culture and nature trips to southern Mexico. The company can also prepare custom itineraries.

   Culinary Adventures, 6023 Reid Dr. NW, Gig Harbor, WA 98335 (© **253/851-7676;** fax 253/851-9532; www.marilyn tausend.com) specializes in a short but select list of cooking tours in Mexico. They feature well-known cooks and travel to regions known for excellent cuisine. The owner, Marilyn Tausend, is the coauthor of *Mexico the Beautiful Cookbook* and *Cocinas de la Familia* (Family Kitchens). Most trips take place in central Mexico, but ask about itineraries in the Yucatán.

   Mexico Travel Link Ltd., 300-3665 Kingsway, Vancouver, BC V5R 5W2 Canada (© **604/454-9044;** fax 604/454-9088; www. mexicotravel.net), offers cultural, sports, and adventure tours to the Maya Route, and other destinations off the beaten path.

   Trek America, P.O. Box 189, Rockaway, NJ 07866 (© **800/221-0596** or 973/983-1144; fax 973/983-8551; www.trekamerica.com), organizes lengthy, active trips that combine trekking, hiking, van transportation, and camping in the Yucatán.

15 Getting Around Cancún

An important note: If your travel schedule depends on a vital connection—say, a plane trip or a ferry or bus connection—call to find out if the connection is still available.

BY PLANE

Mexico has two large private national carriers: **Mexicana** (✆ 01-800/509-8960 toll-free in Mexico), and **AeroMéxico** (✆ 01-800/021-4000 toll-free in Mexico), in addition to several up-and-coming regional and low-cost carriers. Mexicana and AeroMéxico offer extensive connections to the United States as well as within Mexico.

Up-and-coming low-cost carriers include **Aviacsa** (www.aviacsa.com), **Click Mexicana** (www.click.com.mx), and **Interjet** (www.interjet.com.mx). Regional carriers include **Aerovega** (www.aerovega.com), **Aero Tucán** (www.aero-tucan.com), and AeroMéxico's **Aerolitoral** (www.aeroliteral.com.mx). The regional carriers can be expensive, but they go to difficult-to-reach places.

Because major airlines can book some regional carriers, read your ticket carefully to see if your connecting flight is on one of these smaller carriers—they may use a different airport or a different counter.

AIRPORT TAXES   Mexico charges an airport tax on all departures, which is included in the price of plane tickets. Passengers leaving the country on international flights pay roughly $24—in dollars or the peso equivalent. Taxes on each domestic departure within Mexico are around $17, unless you're on a connecting flight and have already paid at the start of the flight.

Mexico also charges an $18 "tourism tax," the proceeds of which go into a tourism promotional fund. Your ticket price may not include it, so be sure to have enough money to pay it at the airport upon departure.

RECONFIRMING FLIGHTS   Although Mexican airlines say it's not necessary to reconfirm a flight, it's still a good idea. To avoid getting bumped on popular, possibly overbooked flights, check in for an international flight at least 2 hours in advance of travel.

BY CAR

Most Mexican roads are not up to U.S. standards. Driving at night is dangerous—the roads are rarely lit; trucks, carts, pedestrians, and bicycles usually have no lights; and you can hit potholes, animals, rocks, dead ends, or uncrossable bridges without warning.

The spirited style of Mexican driving sometimes requires super vision and reflexes. Be prepared for new customs, as when a truck driver flips on his left turn signal when there's not a crossroad for miles. He's probably telling you the road's clear ahead for you to pass. Another custom that's very important to respect is turning left. Never turn left by stopping in the middle of a highway with your left signal on. Instead, pull onto the right shoulder, wait for traffic to clear, then proceed across the road.

GASOLINE   There's one government-owned brand of gas and one gasoline station name throughout the country—**Pemex** (Petroleras Mexicanas). There are two types of gas in Mexico: *magna,* 87-octane unleaded gas, and premium 93 octane. In Mexico, fuel and oil are sold by the liter, which is slightly more than a quart (40 liters equals about 11 gal.). Many franchise Pemex stations have bathroom facilities and convenience stores.

Important note: Pemex stations now accept both credit and debit cards for gas purchases, marking an important change from prior years, although this service is often not available at night, when most stations still accept only cash.

TOLL ROADS   Mexico charges some of the highest tolls in the world for its network of new toll roads; as a result, they are rarely used. Generally speaking, though, using toll roads cuts travel time. Older toll-free roads are generally in good condition, but travel times tend to be longer.

BREAKDOWNS   If your car breaks down on the road, help might already be on the way. Radio-equipped green repair trucks operated by uniformed English-speaking officers patrol major highways during daylight hours. These **"Green Angels"** perform minor repairs and adjustments free, but you pay for parts and materials.

Your best guide to repair shops is the Yellow Pages. For repairs, look under "Automóviles y Camiones: Talleres de Reparación y Servicio"; auto-parts stores are under "Refacciones y Accesorios para Automóviles." To find a mechanic on the road, look for a sign that says TALLER MECANICO.

Places called *vulcanizadora* or *llantera* repair flat tires, and it is common to find them open 24 hours a day on the most traveled highways.

MINOR ACCIDENTS   When possible, many Mexicans drive away from minor accidents, or try to make an immediate settlement, to avoid involving the police. If the police arrive while the involved persons are still at the scene, everyone may be locked in jail until blame is assessed. In any case, you have to settle up immediately, which may take days. Foreigners who don't speak fluent Spanish are at a distinct disadvantage when trying to explain their version of the event. Three steps may help the foreigner who doesn't wish to do as the Mexicans do: If you were in your own car, notify your Mexican insurance company, whose job it is to intervene on your behalf. If you were in a rental car, notify the rental company immediately and ask how to contact the nearest adjuster. (You did buy insurance with the rental, right?) Finally, if all else fails, ask for the nearest Green Angel, who may be able to explain to officials that you are covered by insurance.

CAR RENTALS   You'll get the best price if you reserve a car at least a week in advance in the United States. U.S. car-rental firms include **Advantage** (© 800/777-5500 in the U.S. and Canada; www.arac.com), **Avis** (© 800/331-1212 in the U.S., 800/TRY-AVIS in Canada; www.avis.com), **Budget** (© 800/527-0700 in the U.S. and Canada; www.budget.com), **Hertz** (© 800/654-3131 in the U.S. and Canada; www.hertz.com), **National** (© 800/CAR-RENT in the U.S. and Canada; www.nationalcar.com), and **Thrifty** (© 800/847-4389 in the U.S. and Canada; www.thrifty.com), which often offers discounts for rentals in Mexico. For European travelers, **Kemwel Holiday Auto** (© 800/678-0678; www.kemwel.com) and **Auto Europe** (© 800/223-5555; www.autoeurope.com) can arrange Mexican rentals, sometimes through other agencies. These and some local firms have offices in Mexico City and most other large Mexican cities. You'll find rental desks at airports, all major hotels, and many travel agencies.

Cars are easy to rent if you are 25 or over and have a major credit card, valid driver's license, and passport with you. Without a credit card, you must leave a cash deposit, usually a big one. One-way rentals are usually simple to arrange but more costly.

Car-rental costs are high in Mexico because cars are more expensive. The condition of rental cars has improved greatly over the years, and clean new cars are the norm. You will pay the least for a manual car without air-conditioning. Prices may be considerably higher if you rent around a major holiday. Also double-check charges for insurance—some companies will increase the insurance rate after several days. Always ask for detailed information about all charges you will be responsible for.

Car-rental companies usually write credit card charges in U.S. dollars.

Deductibles   Be careful—these vary greatly; some are as high as $2,500, which comes out of your pocket immediately in case of damage.

Insurance   Insurance is offered in two parts: **Collision and damage** insurance covers your car and others if the accident is your fault, and **personal accident** insurance covers you and anyone in your car. Read the fine print on the back of your rental agreement and note that insurance may be invalid if you have an accident while driving on an unpaved road.

Damage   Always inspect your car carefully and note every damaged or missing item, no matter how minute, on your rental agreement, or you may be charged.

BY TAXI

Taxis are the preferred way to get around Cancún. Fares for short trips within towns are generally preset by zone, and are quite reasonable compared with U.S. rates. For longer trips or excursions to nearby cities, radio taxis can generally be hired for around $10 to $15 per hour, or for a negotiated daily rate. A negotiated one-way price is usually much less than the cost of a rental car for a day, and a taxi travels much faster than a bus. For anyone who is uncomfortable driving in Mexico, this is a convenient, comfortable alternative. A bonus is that you have a Spanish-speaking person with you in case you run into trouble. Many taxi drivers speak at least some English. For safety reasons, you should request a *sitio* (radio) taxi rather than hailing one off the street. Your hotel can assist you with the arrangements.

BY BUS

Mexican buses run frequently, are readily accessible, and can get you almost anywhere you want to go. They're often the only way to get from large cities to other nearby cities and small villages. Don't hesitate to ask questions if you're confused about anything, but note that little English is spoken in bus stations.

Dozens of Mexican companies operate large, air-conditioned, Greyhound-type buses between most cities. Classes are second *(segunda)*, first *(primera)*, and deluxe *(ejecutiva)*, which goes by a variety of names. Deluxe buses often have fewer seats than regular buses, show video movies, are air-conditioned, and make few stops. Many run express from point to point. They are well worth the few dollars more. In rural areas, buses are often of the school-bus variety, with lots of local color.

Whenever possible, it's best to buy your reserved-seat ticket, often using a computerized system, a day in advance on long-distance routes and especially before holidays. See the appendix for a list of helpful bus terms in Spanish.

16 Tips on Accommodations

MEXICO'S HOTEL RATING SYSTEM

The hotel rating system in Mexico is called "Stars and Diamonds." Hotels may qualify to earn one to five stars, or five diamonds. Many hotels that have excellent standards are not certified, but all rated hotels adhere to strict standards. The guidelines relate to service, facilities, and hygiene more than to prices.

Five-diamond hotels meet the highest requirements for rating: The beds are comfortable, bathrooms are in excellent working order, all facilities are renovated regularly, infrastructure is top-tier, and services and hygiene meet the highest international standards.

Five-star hotels usually offer similar quality, but with lower levels of service and detail in the rooms. For example, a five-star hotel may have less luxurious linens, or perhaps room service for less than 24 hours.

Four-star hotels are less expensive and more basic, but they still guarantee cleanliness and basic services such as hot water and purified drinking water. Three, two-, and one-star hotels are at least working to adhere to certain standards: Bathrooms are cleaned and linens are washed daily, and you can expect a minimum standard of service. Two- and one-star hotels generally provide bottled water rather than purified water.

The nonprofit organization Calidad Mexicana Certificada, A.C., known as **Calmecac** (**www.calmecac.com.mx**), is responsible for hotel ratings. For additional details about the rating system, visit Calmecac's website or www.starsanddiamonds.com.

HOTEL CHAINS

In addition to the major international chains, you'll run across a number of less-familiar brands as you plan your trip to Mexico. They include:

- **Brisas Hotels & Resorts** (www.brisas.com.mx). These were the hotels that originally attracted jet-set travelers to Mexico. Spectacular in a retro way, these properties offer the laid-back luxury that makes a Mexican vacation so unique.

- **Fiesta Americana** and **Fiesta Inn** (www.posadas.com). Part of the Mexican-owned Grupo Posadas company, these hotels set the country's midrange standard for facilities and services. They generally offer comfortable, spacious rooms and traditional Mexican hospitality. Fiesta Americana hotels offer excellent beach-resort packages. Fiesta Inn hotels are usually more business oriented. Grupo Posadas also owns the more luxurious Aqua and Caesar Park hotels and the eco-oriented Explorean hotels.

- **Hoteles Camino Real** (www.caminoreal.com). Once known as the premier Mexican hotel chain, Camino Real still maintains a high standard of service at its properties, although the company was sold in 2005, and many of the hotels that once formed a part of it have been sold off, or have become independent. Its beach hotels are traditionally located on the best beaches in the area. This chain also focuses on the business market. The hotels are famous for their vivid and contrasting colors.

- **NH Hoteles** (www.nh-hoteles.com). The NH hotels are noted for their family-friendly facilities and quality standards. The beach properties' signature feature is a pool, framed by columns, overlooking the sea.

- **Quinta Real Grand Class Hotels and Resorts** (www.quinta real.com). These hotels, owned by Summit Hotels and Resorts, are noted for architectural and cultural details that reflect their individual regions. At these luxury properties, attention to detail and excellent service are the rule.

HOUSE RENTALS & SWAPS

House and villa rentals and swaps are becoming more common in Mexico, but no single recognized agency or business provides this service exclusively for Mexico. In the chapters that follow, we have provided information on independent services that we have found to be reputable.

With regard to general online services, the most extensive inventory of homes is found at **VRBO** (Vacation Rentals by Owner; www.vrbo.com). They have over 33,000 homes and condominiums worldwide, including a large selection in Mexico. Another good option is **VacationSpot** (© 888/903-7768; www.vacationspot. com) owned by Expedia.com, and a part of its sister company, Hotels.com. It has fewer choices, but the company's criteria for

---

Finds **Out-of-the-Ordinary Places to Stay**

Mexico Boutique Hotels (www.mexicoboutiquehotels.com) specializes in smaller places to stay with a high level of personal attention and service. Most options have fewer than 50 rooms, and the accommodations consist of entire villas, *casitas,* bungalows, or a combination. The Yucatán is especially noted for luxury haciendas throughout the peninsula.

---

adding inventory are much more selective, and often include on-site inspections. They also offer toll-free phone support.

You might also consider trying **HomeLink International** (www. homelink.org), the largest and oldest home-swapping organization, founded in 1952, with over 11,000 listings worldwide ($90 for a yearly membership). **HomeExchange.org** and **InterVac.com** are also reliable.

SURFING FOR HOTELS

In addition to the online travel booking sites **Travelocity, Expedia, Orbitz, Priceline,** and **Hotwire**, you can book hotels through **Hotels.com; Quikbook** (www.quikbook.com); and **Travelaxe** (www.travelaxe.net).

HotelChatter.com is a daily webzine offering smart coverage and critiques of hotels worldwide. Go to **TripAdvisor.com** or **HotelShark.com** for helpful independent consumer reviews of hotels and resort properties.

It's a good idea to **get a confirmation number** and **make a printout** of any online booking transaction.

LANDING THE BEST ROOM

Somebody has to get the best room in the house, and it might as well be you. You can start by joining the hotel's frequent-guest program, which may make you eligible for upgrades. Always ask about a corner room. They're often larger and quieter, with more windows and light, and they often cost the same as standard rooms. When you make your reservation, ask if the hotel is renovating; if it is, request a room away from the construction. Ask about nonsmoking rooms, rooms with views, rooms with twin, queen-, or king-size beds. If you're a light sleeper, request a quiet room away from vending machines, elevators, restaurants, bars, and dance clubs. Ask for a room that has been most recently renovated or redecorated.

In resort areas, ask the following questions before you book a room:

- What's the view like?
- Does the room have air-conditioning or ceiling fans? Do the windows open? If they do, and the nighttime entertainment takes place alfresco, you may want to find out when showtime is over.
- What's included in the price?
- How far is the room from the beach and other amenities? If it's far, is there transportation and is it free?

17 Tips on Dining

Authentic Mexican food differs dramatically from what is frequently served in the United States under that name. For many travelers, even Cancún will be new and exciting culinary territory. Even grizzled veterans will be pleasantly surprised by the wide variation in specialties and traditions offered from region to region.

Despite regional differences, some generalizations can be made. Mexican food usually isn't pepper-hot when it arrives at the table (though many dishes must have a certain amount of piquancy, and some home cooking can be very spicy, depending on a family's or chef's tastes). Chiles and sauces add piquant flavor after the food is served; you'll never see a table in Mexico without one or both of these condiments. Mexicans don't drown their cooking in cheese and sour cream, a la Tex-Mex, and they use a great variety of ingredients. But the basis of Mexican food is simple—tortillas, beans, chiles, squash, and tomatoes—the same as it was centuries ago, before the Europeans arrived.

THE BASICS

TORTILLAS Traditional tortillas are made from corn that's boiled in water and lime, and then ground into *masa* (a grainy dough), patted and pressed into thin cakes, and cooked on a hot griddle known as a *comal.* In many households, the tortilla takes the place of fork and spoon; Mexicans merely tear them into wedge-shaped pieces, which they use to scoop up their food. Restaurants often serve bread rather than tortillas because it's easier, but you can always ask for tortillas. A more recent invention from northern Mexico is the flour tortilla, which is seen less frequently in the rest of Mexico.

ENCHILADAS The tortilla is the basis of several Mexican dishes, but the most famous of these is the enchilada. The original name for this dish would have been *tortilla enchilada*, which simply means a tortilla dipped in a chile sauce. In like manner, there's the *entomatada* (tortilla dipped in a tomato sauce) and the *enfrijolada* (a bean sauce). The enchilada began as a very simple dish: A tortilla is dipped in chile sauce (usually with ancho chile) and then into very hot oil, and then is quickly folded or rolled on a plate and sprinkled with chopped onions and a little *queso cotija* (crumbly white cheese) and served with a few fried potatoes and carrots. You can get this basic enchilada in food stands across the country. I love them, and if you come across them in your travels, give them a try. In restaurants you get the more elaborate enchilada, with different fillings of cheese, chicken, pork, or even seafood, and sometimes in a casserole.

TACOS   A taco is anything folded or rolled into a tortilla, and sometimes a double tortilla. The tortilla can be served either soft or fried. Flautas and quesadillas are species of tacos. For Mexicans, the taco is the quintessential fast food, and the taco stand *(taquería)*—a ubiquitous sight—is a great place to get a filling meal. See the section "Eating Out: Restaurants, *Taquerías* & Tipping," below, for information on taquerías.

FRIJOLES   An invisible "bean line" divides Mexico: It starts at the Gulf Coast in the southern part of the state of Tamaulipas and moves inland through the eastern quarter of San Luis Potosí and most of the state of Hidalgo, then goes straight through Mexico City and Morelos and into Guerrero, where it curves slightly westward to the Pacific. To the north and west of this line, the pink bean known as the *flor de mayo* is the staple food; to the south and east, including all of the Yucatán, the standard is the black bean.

In private households, beans are served at least once a day and, among the working class and peasantry, with every meal, if the family can afford it. Mexicans almost always prepare beans with a minimum of condiments—usually just a little onion and garlic and perhaps a pinch of herbs. Beans are meant to be a contrast to the heavily spiced dishes. Sometimes they are served at the end of a meal with a little Mexican-style sour cream.

Mexicans often fry leftover beans and serve them on the side as *frijoles refritos*. "Refritos" is usually translated as refried, but this is a misnomer—the beans are fried only once. The prefix "re" actually means "well" (as in thoroughly).

TAMALES   You make a tamal by mixing corn *masa* with a little lard, adding one of several fillings—meats flavored with chiles (or no filling at all)—then wrapping it in a corn husk or in the leaf of a banana or other plant, and finally steaming it. Every region in Mexico has its own traditional way of making tamales. In some places, a single tamale can be big enough to feed a family, while in others they are barely 3 inches long and an inch thick.

CHILES   Many kinds of chile peppers exist, and Mexicans call each of them by one name when they're fresh and another when they're dried. Some are blazing hot with only a mild flavor; some are mild but have a rich, complex flavor. They can be pickled, smoked, stuffed, stewed, chopped, and used in an endless variety of dishes.

MEALTIME

MORNING   The morning meal, known as *el desayuno,* can be something light, such as coffee and sweet bread, or something more substantial: eggs, beans, tortillas, bread, fruit, and juice. It can be eaten early or late and is always a sure bet in Mexico. The variety and sweetness of the fruits is remarkable, and you can't go wrong with Mexican egg dishes.

MIDAFTERNOON   The main meal of the day, known as *la comida* (or *el almuerzo*), is eaten between 2 and 4pm. Stores and businesses often close, and many people go home to eat and perhaps take a short afternoon siesta before going about their business. The first course is the *sopa,* which can be either soup *(caldo)* or rice *(sopa de arroz)* or both; then comes the main course, which ideally is a meat or fish dish prepared in some kind of sauce and served with beans, followed by dessert.

EVENING   Between 8 and 10pm, most Mexicans have a light meal called *la cena.* If eaten at home, it is something like a sandwich, bread and jam, or perhaps a couple of tacos made from some of the day's leftovers. At restaurants, the most common thing to eat is *antojitos* (literally, "little cravings"), a general label for light fare. Antojitos include tostadas, tamales, tacos, and simple enchiladas, which are big hits with travelers. Large restaurants offer complete meals as well.

EATING OUT: RESTAURANTS, *TAQUERIAS* & TIPPING

Avoid eating at those inviting sidewalk restaurants that you see beneath the stone archways that border the main plazas. These places usually cater to tourists and don't need to count on getting any return business. But they are great for getting a coffee or beer.

If you venture outside Cancún, you'll find that most towns have one or two restaurants (sometimes one is a coffee shop) that are social centers for a large group of established patrons. These establishments over time become virtual institutions, and change comes very slowly. The food is usually good standard fare, cooked as it was 20 years ago; the decor is simple. The patrons have known each other and the staff for years, and the *charla* (banter), gestures, and greetings are friendly, open, and unaffected. If you're curious about Mexican culture, eating and observing the goings-on is fun.

During your trip, you're going to see many **taquerías (taco joints).** These are generally small places with a counter or a few tables set around the cooking area; you get to see exactly how the cooks make their tacos before deciding whether to order. Most tacos come with a little chopped onion and cilantro, but not tomato and lettuce. Find one that seems popular with the locals and where the cook performs with brio (a good sign of pride in the product). Sometimes a woman will be making the tortillas right there (or working the *masa* into *gorditas, sopes,* or *panuchos,* if these are also served). You will never see men doing this—this is perhaps the strictest gender division in Mexican society. Men may do all other cooking and kitchen tasks, and work with prepared tortillas, but they will never be found working *masa.*

For the main meal of the day, many restaurants offer a multi-course blue-plate special called *comida corrida* or *menú del día.* This is the least expensive way to get a full dinner. In Mexico, you need to ask for your check; it is generally considered inhospitable to present a check to someone who hasn't requested it. If you're in a hurry to get somewhere, ask for the check when your food arrives.

Tips are about the same as in the United States. You'll sometimes find a 15% **value-added tax** on restaurant meals, which shows up on the bill as "IVA." This is a boon to arithmetically challenged tippers, saving them from undue exertion.

To summon the waiter, wave or raise your hand, but don't motion with your index finger, which is a demeaning gesture that may even cause the waiter to ignore you. Or if it's the check you want, you can motion to the waiter from across the room using the universal pretend-you're-writing gesture.

Most restaurants do not have **nonsmoking sections;** when they do, we mention it in the reviews. But Mexico's wonderful climate allows for many open-air restaurants, usually set inside a courtyard of a colonial house, or in rooms with tall ceilings and plenty of open windows.

DRINKS

All over Mexico you'll find shops selling *jugos* (juices) and *licuados* (smoothies) made from several kinds of tropical fruit. They're excellent and refreshing; while traveling, I take full advantage of them. You'll also come across *aguas frescas*—water flavored with hibiscus, melon, tamarind, or lime. Soft drinks come in more flavors than in any other country I know. Pepsi and Coca-Cola taste the way they did in the United States years ago, before the makers started adding corn syrup. The coffee is generally good, and **hot chocolate** is a traditional drink, as is *atole*—a hot, corn-based beverage that can be sweet or bitter.

Of course, Mexico has a proud and lucrative **beer**-brewing tradition. A lesser-known brewed beverage is *pulque,* a pre-Hispanic drink: the fermented juice of a few species of maguey or agave. Mostly you find it for sale in *pulquerías* in central Mexico. It is an acquired taste, and not every gringo acquires it. **Mezcal** and **tequila** also come from the agave. Tequila is a variety of mezcal produced from the *A. tequilana* species of agave in and around the area of Tequila, in the state of Jalisco. Mezcal comes from various parts of Mexico and from different varieties of agave. The distilling process is usually much less sophisticated than that of tequila, and, with its stronger smell and taste, mezcal is much more easily detected on the drinker's breath. In some places such as Oaxaca and Guerrero, it comes with a worm in the bottle; you are supposed to eat the worm after polishing off the mezcal. But for those of you teetotalers out there who are interested in just the worm, I have good news—you can find them for sale in Mexican markets when in season. *¡Salud!*

FAST FACTS: Cancún

Abbreviations Dept. (apartments); Apdo. (post office box); Av. (*avenida;* avenue); c/ (*calle;* street); Calz. (*calzada;* boulevard). "C" on faucets stands for *caliente* (hot), "F" for *fría* (cold). "PB" *(planta baja)* means ground floor; in most buildings the next floor up is the first floor (1).

American Express The local office is at Av. Tulum 208 and Agua (© **998/881-4000** or -4055; www.americanexpress.com/mexico), 1 block past the Plaza México. It's open Monday through Friday from 9am to 6pm, Saturday from 9am to 1pm.

Area Code The telephone area code is **998**.

ATMs See "Banks & ATMs," p. 12.

Climate It's hot but not overwhelmingly humid. The rainy season is May through October. August through October is hurricane season, which brings erratic weather. November through February is generally sunny but can also be cloudy, windy, somewhat rainy, and even cool.

Consulates The **U.S. Consular Agent** is in the Plaza Caracol 2, Bulevar Kukulkán Km 8.5, 3rd level, 320–323 (© **998/883-0272**). The office is open Monday through Friday from 9am to 2pm. The **Canadian Consulate** is in the Plaza Caracol, 3rd level, Loc. 330 (© **998/883-3360**). The office is open Monday through Friday from 9am to 5pm. The **United Kingdom** has a consular office at the Royal Sands Hotel in Cancún (© **998/881-0100**, ext. 65898; fax 998/848-8662; information@britishconsulateCancun.com). The office is open Monday through Friday from 9am to 3pm. Irish, Australian, and New Zealand citizens should contact their embassies in Mexico City.

Crime Car break-ins are just about the only crime here. They happen frequently, especially around the shopping centers in the Hotel Zone. VW Beetles and Golfs are frequent targets.

Currency Exchange Most banks sit downtown along Avenida Tulum and are usually open Monday through Friday from 9:30am to 4pm. Many have automated teller machines for after-hours cash withdrawals. In the Hotel Zone, you'll find banks in the Kukulcán Plaza and next to the convention center. There are also many *casas de cambio* (exchange houses). Downtown merchants are eager to change cash dollars, but island stores don't offer very good exchange rates. Avoid changing money at the airport as you arrive, especially at the first exchange booth you see—its rates are less favorable than those of any in town or others farther inside the airport concourse.

Cameras & Film Film costs about the same as in the United States. It is never considered polite to take photos inside a church in Mexico.

Car Rentals See "Getting Around Cancún," p. 36.

Customs What You Can Bring Into Mexico When you enter Mexico, Customs officials will be tolerant as long as you have no illegal drugs or firearms. Tourists are allowed to bring in their personal effects duty-free. A laptop computer, camera equipment, and sports equipment that could feasibly be used during your stay are also allowed. The underlying guideline is: Don't bring anything that looks as if it's meant to be resold in Mexico. **U.S. citizens** entering Mexico by the land border can bring in gifts worth a value of up to $50 duty-free, except for alcohol and tobacco products. Those entering Mexico by air or sea can bring in gifts worth a value of up to $300 duty-free. The **website for Mexican Customs** (*Aduanas*) is: www.aduanas. sat.gob.mx/webadunet/body.htm.

Customs What You Can Take Home From Mexico
U.S. Citizens: For specifics on what you can bring back and the corresponding fees, download the invaluable free pamphlet *Know Before You Go* online at **www.cbp.gov**. (Click on "Travel," and then click on "Know Before You Go! Online Brochure") Or contact the **U.S. Customs & Border Protection (CBP)**, 1300 Pennsylvania Ave., NW, Washington, DC 20229 (© 877/287-8667) and request the pamphlet.

   Canadian Citizens: For a clear summary of Canadian rules, write for the booklet *I Declare*, issued by the **Canada Border Services Agency** (© 800/461-9999 in Canada, or 204/983-3500; **www.cbsa-asfc.gc.ca**).

   U.K. Citizens: For information, contact **HM Customs & Excise** at © 0845/010-9000 (from outside the U.K., 020/8929-0152), or consult their website at **www.hmce.gov.uk**.

   Australian Citizens: A helpful brochure available from Australian consulates or Customs offices is *Know Before You Go*. For more information, call the **Australian Customs Service** at © 1300/363-263, or log on to **www.customs.gov.au**.

   New Zealand Citizens: Most questions are answered in a free pamphlet available at New Zealand consulates and Customs offices: *New Zealand Customs Guide for Travellers, Notice no. 4*. For more information, contact **New Zealand Customs**, The Customhouse, 17–21 Whitmore St., Box 2218, Wellington (© 04/473-6099 or 0800/428-786; **www.customs.govt.nz**).

Drug Laws It may sound obvious, but don't use or possess illegal drugs in Mexico. Mexican officials have no tolerance for drug users, and jail is their solution, with very little hope of getting out until the sentence (usually a long one) is completed or heavy fines or bribes are paid. Remember, in Mexico the legal system assumes you are guilty until proven innocent. *Note:* It isn't uncommon to be befriended by a fellow user, only to be turned in by that "friend," who collects a bounty.

Bring prescription drugs in their original containers. If possible, pack a copy of the original prescription with the generic name of the drug.

U.S. Customs officials are on the lookout for diet drugs that are sold in Mexico but illegal in the U.S. Possession could land you in a U.S. jail. If you buy antibiotics over-the-counter (which you can do in Mexico) and still have some left, U.S. Customs probably won't hassle you.

Drugstores Across the street from Señor Frog's in the Hotel Zone, at Bulevar Kukulkán Km 9.5, **Farmacías del Ahorro** (© **998/892-7291**) offers 24 hour service and free delivery. Plenty of drugstores are in the major shopping malls in the Hotel Zone, and are open until 10pm. In downtown Cancún, **Farmacía Cancún** is located at Av. Tulum 17 (© **998/884-1283**). You can stock up on over-the-counter and many prescription drugs without a prescription.

Electricity The electrical system in Mexico is 110 volts AC (60 cycles), as in the United States and Canada. In reality, however, it may cycle more slowly and overheat your appliances. To compensate, select a medium or low speed on hair dryers. Many older hotels still have electrical outlets for flat two-prong plugs; you'll need an adapter for any plug with an enlarged end on one prong or with three prongs. Many better hotels have three-hole outlets (*trifásicos* in Spanish). Those that don't may have loan adapters, but to be sure, it's always better to carry your own.

Embassies & Consulates There is a U.S. consular agency in Cancún (see "Consulates," above). The Embassy of the **United States** in Mexico City is at Paseo de la Reforma 305, next to the Hotel María Isabel Sheraton at the corner of Río Danubio (© **55/5080-2000** or 5511-9980); hours are Monday through Friday from 8:30am to 5:30pm. Visit www.usembassy-mexico. gov for addresses of the U.S. consulates inside Mexico.

The Embassy of **Australia** in Mexico City is at Rubén Darío 55, Col. Polanco (© **55/51101-2200**). It's open Monday through Friday from 9am-to 1pm.

The Embassy of **Canada** in Mexico City is at Schiller 529, Col. Polanco (© **55/5724-7900**); it's open Monday through Friday from 9am to 1pm. At other times, the name of a duty officer is posted on the door. Visit www.dfait-maeci.gc.ca for addresses of consular agencies in Mexico.

The Embassy of **New Zealand** in Mexico City is at Jaime Balmes 8, 4th floor, Col. Los Morales, Polanco (🕿 55/5283-9460; kiwimexico@compuserve.com.mx). It's open Monday through Thursday from 8:30am to 2pm and 3 to 5:30pm, and Friday from 8:30am to 2pm.

The Embassy of the **United Kingdom** in Mexico City is at Río Lerma 71, Col. Cuauhtémoc (🕿 55/5242-8500; www.embajada britanica.com.mx). It's open Monday through Friday from 8:30am to 3:30pm.

The Embassy of **Ireland** in Mexico City is at Bulevar Cerrada, Avila Camacho 76, 3rd floor, Col. Lomas de Chapultepec (🕿 55/5520-5803). It's open Monday through Friday from 9am to 5pm.

The **South African** Embassy in Mexico City is at Andrés Bello 10, 9th floor, Col. Polanco (🕿 55/5282-9260). It's open Monday through Friday from 8am to 4pm.

Emergencies To report an emergency, dial 🕿 **060,** which is supposed to be similar to 911 emergency service in the United States. For first aid, the **Cruz Roja,** or Red Cross (🕿 **065** or 998/ 884-1616; fax 998/883-9218), is open 24 hours on Avenida Yax-chilán between avenidas Xcaret and Labná, next to the Telmex building. **Total Assist,** Claveles 5, SM 22, at Avenida Tulum (🕿 **998/884-8022;** totalassist@prodigy.net.mx), is a small (nine-room) emergency hospital with English-speaking doctors. It's open 24 hours and accepts American Express, Master Card, and Visa. Desk staff may have limited command of English. **Air Ambulance** (Global Ambulance) service is avail-able by calling 🕿 **01-800/305-9400** in Mexico.

Internet Access **Alienet** in a kiosk on the second floor of Kukulcán Plaza, Bulevar Kukulkán Km 13 (🕿 **998/840-6099**), offers Internet access for $7 per hour. It's open daily from 10am to 10pm.

Liquor Laws The legal drinking age in Mexico is 18; however, asking for ID or denying purchase is extremely rare. Grocery stores sell everything from beer and wine to national and imported liquors. You can buy liquor 24 hours a day, but dur-ing major elections, dry laws often are enacted for as much as 72 hours in advance of the election—and they apply to tourists as well as local residents. Mexico does not have laws that apply to transporting liquor in cars, but authorities are beginning to target drunk drivers more aggressively. It's a good idea to drive defensively.

It is not legal to drink in the street; however, many tourists do so. Use your judgment—if you are getting drunk, you shouldn't drink in the street, because you are more likely to get stopped by the police.

Luggage Storage & Lockers Hotels will generally tag and store luggage while you travel elsewhere.

Mail Postage for a postcard or letter is 8 pesos; it may arrive anywhere from 1 to 6 weeks later. The price for registered letters and packages depends on the weight, and unreliable delivery time can take 2 to 6 weeks. The recommended way to send a package or important mail is through FedEx, DHL, UPS, or another reputable international mail service.

Newspapers & Magazines Most hotel gift shops and newsstands carry English-language magazines and English-language Mexican newspapers, such as the *Miami Herald.*

Police Cancún has a fleet of English-speaking tourist police to help travelers. Dial ℂ **998/885-2277.** The **Procuraduría Federal del Consumidor (consumer protection agency),** Av. Cobá 9–11 (ℂ **998/884-2634** or -2701), is opposite the Social Security Hospital and upstairs from the Fenix drugstore. It's open Monday through Friday from 9am to 3pm.

Passports **For Residents of the United States:** Whether you're applying in person or by mail, you can download passport applications from the U.S. Department of State website at **http://travel.state.gov**. To find your regional passport office, either check the U.S. Department of State website or call the **National Passport Information Center** toll-free number (ℂ **877/487-2778**) for automated information.

For Residents of Canada: Passport applications are available at travel agencies throughout Canada or from the central **Passport Office,** Department of Foreign Affairs and International Trade, Ottawa, ON K1A 0G3 (ℂ **800/567-6868;** www.ppt.gc.ca).

For Residents of the United Kingdom: To pick up an application for a standard 10-year passport (5-year passport for children younger than 16), visit your nearest passport office, major post office, or travel agency or contact the **United Kingdom Identity & Passport Service** at ℂ **0870/521-0410** or search its website at **www.ukpa.gov.uk**.

For Residents of Ireland: You can apply for a 10-year passport at the **Passport Office,** Setanta Centre, Molesworth Street, Dublin 2 (ℂ **01/671-1633**; www.irlgov.ie/iveagh). Those younger than age 18 and older than 65 must apply for a €12 3-year passport. You can also apply at 1A South Mall, Cork (© 021/272-525) or at most main post offices.

For Residents of Australia: You can pick up an application from your local post office or any branch of Passports Australia, but you must schedule an interview at the passport office to present your application materials. Call the **Australian Passport Information Service** at © **131-232,** or visit the government website at **www.passports.gov.au**.

For Residents of New Zealand: You can pick up a passport application at any New Zealand Passports Office or download it from their website. Contact the **Passports Office** at © **0800/ 225-050** in New Zealand or 04/474-8100, or log on to **www. passports.govt.nz**.

Post Office The main *correo* lies at the intersection of avenidas Sunyaxchen and Xel-Ha (© **998/884-1418**). It's open Monday through Friday from 9am to 4pm, and Saturday from 9am to noon for the purchase of stamps only.

Safety Aside from car break-ins, there is very little crime in Cancún. People are generally safe late at night in tourist areas; just use ordinary common sense. As at any other beach resort, don't take money or valuables to the beach. See "Crime," above.

Swimming on the Caribbean side presents a danger because of the undertow. See the information on beaches in "Beaches, Watersports & Boat Tours" in chapter 3 for information about flag warnings.

Seasons Technically, high season runs from December 15 to April; low season extends from May to December 15, when prices drop 10% to 30%. Some hotels are starting to charge high-season rates during June and July, when Mexican, European, and school-holiday visitors often travel, although rates may still be lower than in winter months.

Smoking Smoking is permitted and generally accepted in most public places, including restaurants, bars, and hotel lobbies. Nonsmoking areas and hotel rooms for nonsmokers are becoming more common in higher-end establishments, but they tend to be the exception rather than the rule.

Special Events The annual **Mexico-Caribbean Food Festival,** featuring special menus of culinary creations throughout town, is held each year between September and November.

Additional information is available through the State Tourism Office.

Taxes The 15% IVA (value-added) tax applies on goods and services in most of Mexico, and it's supposed to be included in the posted price. This tax is 10% in Cancún, Cozumel, and Los Cabos. There is a 5% tax on food and drinks consumed in restaurants that sell alcoholic beverages with an alcohol content of more than 10%; this tax applies whether you drink alcohol or not. Tequila is subject to a 25% tax. Mexico imposes an exit tax of around $24 on every foreigner leaving the country, as well as a tourism tax of $18 (see "Airport Taxes" under "Getting Around Cancún: By Plane," earlier in this chapter).

Telephone & Fax Mexico's telephone system is slowly but surely catching up with modern times. All telephone numbers have 10 digits. Cancún has a three-digit area code (998). To place a local call, you do not need to dial the area code. Many fax numbers are also regular telephone numbers; ask whoever answers for the fax tone *("me da tono de fax, por favor")*. Cellular phones are very popular for small businesses in resort areas and smaller communities. To call a cellular number inside the same area code, dial 044 and then the number. To dial the cellular phone from anywhere else in Mexico, first dial 01, and then the three-digit area code and the seven-digit number. To dial it from the U.S., dial 011-52, plus the three-digit area code and the seven-digit number.

The **country code** for Mexico is **52**. The area code for **Cancún** is **998**.

To call Mexico: If you're calling Mexico from the United States:
1. Dial the international access code: 011.
2. Dial the country code: 52.
3. Dial the two- or three-digit area code, then the eight- or seven-digit number.

To make international calls: To make international calls from Mexico, first dial 00, then the country code (U.S. or Canada 1, U.K. 44, Ireland 353, Australia 61, New Zealand 64). Next, dial the area code and number. For example, to call the British Embassy in Washington, you would dial 00-1-202-588-7800.

For directory assistance: Dial © 040 if you're looking for a number inside Mexico. *Note:* Listings usually appear under the owner's name, not the name of the business, and your chances to find an English-speaking operator are slim to none.

For operator assistance: If you need operator assistance in making a call, dial **090** to make an international call, and **020** to call a number in Mexico.

Toll-free numbers: Numbers beginning with 800 within Mexico are toll-free, but calling a U.S. toll-free number from Mexico costs the same as an overseas call. To call an 800 number in the U.S., dial 001-880 and the last seven digits of the toll-free number. To call an 888 number in the U.S., dial 001-881 and the last seven digits of the toll-free number. For a number with an 887 prefix, dial 882; for 866, dial 883.

Tipping Most service employees count on tips for the majority of their income, and this is especially true for bellboys and waiters. Bellboys should receive the equivalent of 50¢ to $1 (Þ25–55) per bag; waiters generally receive 10% to 20%, depending on the level of service. It is not customary to tip taxi drivers, unless they are hired by the hour or provide touring or other special services.

Water Most hotels have decanters or bottles of purified water in the rooms, and the better hotels have either purified water from regular taps or special taps marked *agua purificada*. Some hotels charge for in-room bottled water. Virtually any hotel, restaurant, or bar will bring you purified water if you specifically request it but will usually charge you for it. Drugstores and grocery stores sell bottled purified water. Some popular brands are Santa María, Ciel, and Bonafont. Evian and other imported brands are also widely available.

2

Where to Stay & Dine in Cancún

Cancún turns 33 in 2008, and, like many 30-somethings, the town is just hitting its prime. In 1974, a group of Mexican government computer analysts picked Cancún for tourism development due to its ideal mix of elements: transparent blue oceans, powdery white beaches, and immense potential for growth. Since then, the city has faced considerable natural challenges, emerging stronger and more irresistible each time. The wreckage of Hurricane Wilma, which tore through the Yucatán Peninsula in 2005, has been replaced by exacting renovations, luxurious upgrades, and brand-new destinations throughout this slice of Caribbean paradise.

Cancún (or "golden snake" in Mayan) stretches from the old city to a 24km (15-mile) sliver of land connected to the mainland by two bridges. Between the old and the new rests the expansive Nichupté lagoon, a lush reminder of Cancún's jungle past.

Cancún remains Mexico's calling card to the world, perfectly showcasing both the country's breathtaking natural beauty and the depth of its 1,000-year history. One astonishing statistic suggests that more Americans travel to Cancún than to any other overseas destination in the world. Indeed, almost three million people visit this enticing beach resort annually—most of them on their first trip to Mexico.

The reasons for Cancún's allure have not changed since the government turned this once isolated beach into a five-star destination. In addition to its stunning coastline, Cancún also offers the highest quality accommodations and easy access by air. While it embodies Caribbean splendor and the exotic joys of Mexico, even a traveler feeling apprehensive about visiting foreign soil will feel completely at ease here. English is spoken and dollars accepted; roads are well-paved and lawns manicured. Most travelers feel comfortable in Cancún, while some also feel surprised to find that it almost resembles a U.S. beach resort more than authentic Mexico. Indeed, signs of Americanism are everywhere here.

In addition to attractions of its own, Cancún is a convenient distance from the more traditional resorts of Isla Mujeres and the coastal zone now known as the Riviera Maya—extending down from Cancún, through Playa del Carmen, to the Maya ruins at Tulum, Cozumel, Chichén Itzá, and Cobá. All lie within day-trip distance.

Cancún's luxury hotels have pools so spectacular that you may find it tempting to remain poolside, but don't. Set aside some time to simply gaze into the ocean and wriggle your toes in the fine, brilliantly white sand. It is, after all, what put Cancún on the map—and not even a tempest of nature has been able to take that away.

1 Where to Stay

Island hotels—almost all of them offering modern facilities and English-speaking staffs—line the beach like concrete dominoes. Extravagance is the byword in the newer hotels. Some hotels, while exclusive, affect a more relaxed attitude. The water on the upper end of the island facing Bahía de Mujeres is placid, while beaches lining the long side of the island facing the Caribbean are subject to choppier water and crashing waves on windy days. (For more information on swimming safety, see "Beaches, Watersports & Boat Tours," in chapter 3.) Be aware that the farther south you go on the island, the longer it takes (20–30 min. in traffic) to get back to the "action spots," which are primarily between the Plaza Flamingo and Punta Cancún on the island and along Avenida Tulum on the mainland.

Following Hurricane Wilma's devastation, the news item that received the most coverage was the destruction of Cancún's famed white-sand beaches, certainly key to selecting a hotel location for many. Immediately following the storm, literally all of the sand was washed away from the northern border of Isla Cancún and Punta Cancún. However, thanks in part to Mother Nature, and in part to a more than $20-million effort by Mexico's government to pump the dislocated sand back to the beach, by spring of 2006, this was no longer an issue. The southern beaches of Isla Cancún actually benefited from the storm, and those areas enjoyed especially wide beachfronts.

Almost all major hotel chains are represented on Cancún Island, so this list can be viewed as a representative summary, with a select number of notable places. The reality is that Cancún is so popular as a package destination from the U.S. that prices and special deals are often the deciding factor for those traveling here (see "Packages for the Independent Traveler," in chapter 1). Ciudad Cancún offers independently owned, smaller, less-expensive lodging; prices are lower here off season (May to early Dec). For condo, home, and villa rentals, check with **Cancún Hideaways** (© **817/522-4466;** fax 817/557-3483; www.cancun-hideaways.com), a company specializing in luxury properties, downtown apartments, and condos— many at prices much lower than comparable hotel stays. Owner Maggie Rodriguez, a former resident of Cancún, has made this niche market her specialty.

The hotel listings in this chapter begin on Cancún Island and finish in Cancún City (the real downtown), where bargain lodgings are available. Parking is free at all island hotels.

CANCUN ISLAND
VERY EXPENSIVE
Fiesta Americana Grand Coral Beach ✸✸✸   This spectacular hotel, which opened in 1991, has one of the best locations in Cancún, with 300m (984 ft.) of prime beachfront and proximity to the main shopping and entertainment centers. The all-suites hotel includes junior suites with sunken sitting areas, whitewashed furniture, marble bathrooms, and soothing California colors. Service throughout this five-diamond property is gracious and attentive, and the expansive lobby is embellished with elegant dark-green granite and an abundance of marble. The hotel's great Punta Cancún location (opposite the Cancún Center) has the advantage of facing the beach to the north, meaning that the surf is calm and perfect for swimming.

Bulevar Kukulkán Km 9.5, 77500 Cancún, Q. Roo. © **800/343-7821** in the U.S., or 998/881-3200. Fax 998/881-3273. www.fiestaamericana.com. 602 units. High season $519 (£285) and up double, $639 (£351) and up club-floor double; low season $339 (£186) and up double, $459 (£252) and up club-floor double. AE, MC, V. **Amenities:** 3 restaurants; poolside snack bar; 5 bars; outdoor pool w/swim-up bars; 3 indoor tennis courts; fitness center; sauna; watersports equipment/rentals; concierge; travel agency; car-rental desk; business center; salon; room service; massage; babysitting; laundry service; concierge floor. *In room:* A/C, TV, minibar, hair dryer, coffeemaker, iron, safe.

Hilton Cancún Beach & Golf Resort ✸✸ *Kids*   Grand, expansive, and fully equipped, this is a true resort in every sense of the word. The Hilton Cancún sits on 100 hectares (247 acres) of prime beachside property, a location that gives every room a sea view (some have both sea and lagoon views), with an 18-hole par-72 golf

Where to Stay & Dine in Downtown Cancún

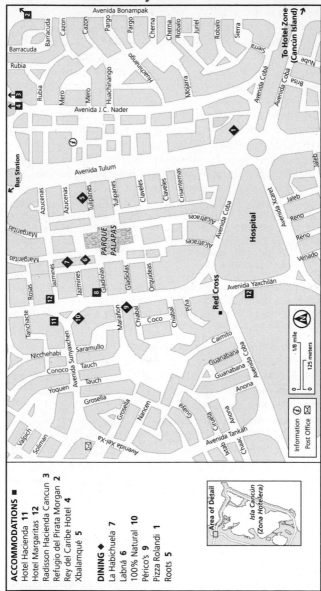

ACCOMMODATIONS ■
Hotel Hacienda 11
Hotel Margaritas 12
Radisson Hacienda Cancun 3
Refugio del Pirata Morgan 2
Rey del Caribe Hotel 4
Xbalamqué 5

DINING ◆
La Habichuela 7
Labná 6
100% Natural 10
Périco's 9
Pizza Rolandi 1
Roots 5

59

course across the street. Like the sprawling resort, rooms are grandly spacious and immaculately decorated in minimalist style, and following Hurricane Wilma, all received an update. It's a very kid-friendly hotel, with one of the island's best children's activity programs, special children's pool, and babysitting available. The hotel's spectacular multisection swimming pool stretches out to the gorgeous beach. The Hilton is especially appealing to golfers because it's one of only two in Cancún with an on-site course (the other is the Meliá). Greens fees for guests are $99 (£54) for 9 holes, $149 (£82) for 18 holes, and include the use of a cart. The Wellness Spa includes oceanfront massage cabañas, yoga, and aromatherapy. This Hilton has a friendly and energetic vibe and boasts wonderful service for such a large resort.

Bulevar Kukulkán Km 17, Retorno Lacandones, 77500 Cancún, Q. Roo. © 800/ 228-3000 in the U.S., or 998/881-8000. Fax 998/881-8080. www.hiltoncancun. com. 426 units. High season $249–$349 (£137–£192) double, $440–$585 (£242–£322) Beach Club double, $555–$779 (£305–£428) suite; low season $119–$300 (£65–£165) double, $350–$550 (£193–£303) Beach Club double, $395–$500 (£217–£275) suite. AE, DC, MC, V. **Amenities:** 5 restaurants; 2 bars; 7 interconnected outdoor pools w/swim-up bar; golf course across the street; golf clinic; 2 lighted tennis courts; Wellness Spa w/spa services and fully equipped gym; 2 whirlpools; watersports center; Kids' Club; concierge; tour desk; car-rental desk; salon; room service; babysitting; laundry service. *In room:* A/C, TV, minibar, coffee-maker, hair dryer, iron, safe, bathrobes.

JW Marriott ♛♛♛ One of Cancún's most upscale and appealing properties, the JW Marriott offers elegance without pretense. From the expansive marble and flower-filled lobby to the luxurious ocean-view guest rooms, the hotel combines classic and Caribbean styling with warm Mexican service. Guest rooms feature beautiful marble bathrooms with separate tub and shower, private balconies, flatscreen TVs, bathrobes and slippers, and twice daily maid service. The inviting free-form infinity pool extends to the white-sand beach, and families feel as comfortable here as romance-seeking couples. A spectacular 3,252-sq.-m (35,000-sq.-ft.) spa includes an indoor pool and Jacuzzi, high-tech fitness center, and full range of massages, body scrubs and polishes, facials, and healing water treatments. **Gustino** is an outstanding Italian restaurant seated off the lobby (see "Where to Dine" later in this chapter), and afternoon tea with a musical trio is offered in the lobby lounge. Guests here also enjoy access to the adjacent Marriott Casa Magna.

Bulevar Kukulkán Km 14.5, 77500 Cancún, Q. Roo. © 800/223-6388 in the U.S., or 998/848-9600. Fax 998/848-9601. www.jwmarriottcancun.com. 448 units. High

Where to Stay & Dine in the Hotel Zone

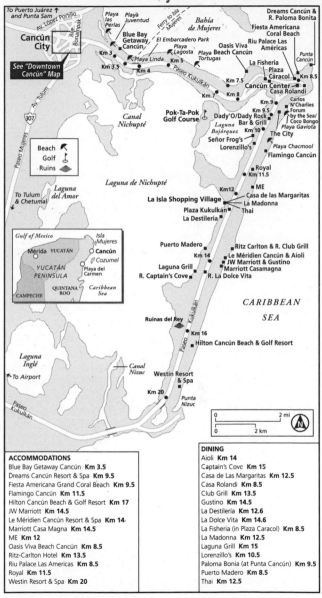

ACCOMMODATIONS
Blue Bay Getaway Cancún **Km 3.5**
Dreams Cancún Resort & Spa **Km 9.5**
Fiesta Americana Grand Coral Beach **Km 9.5**
Flamingo Cancún **Km 11.5**
Hilton Cancún Beach & Golf Resort **Km 17**
JW Marriott **Km 14.5**
Le Méridien Cancún Resort & Spa **Km 14**
Marriott Casa Magna **Km 14.5**
ME **Km 12**
Oasis Viva Beach Cancún **Km 8.5**
Ritz-Carlton Hotel **Km 13.5**
Riu Palace Las Americas **Km 8.5**
Royal **Km 11.5**
Westin Resort & Spa **Km 20**

DINING
Aioli **Km 14**
Captain's Cove **Km 15**
Casa de Las Margaritas **Km 12.5**
Casa Rolandi **Km 8.5**
Club Grill **Km 13.5**
Gustino **Km 14.5**
La Destilería **Km 12.6**
La Dolce Vita **Km 14.6**
La Fisheria (in Plaza Caracol) **Km 8.5**
La Madonna **Km 12.5**
Laguna Grill **Km 15**
Lorenzillo's **Km 10.5**
Paloma Bonia (at Punta Cancún) **Km 9.5**
Puerto Madero **Km 8.5**
Thai **Km 12.5**

season $554–$653 (£305–£359) double; low season $300–$400 (£165–£220) double. AE, DC, MC, V. Small pets allowed with prior reservation. **Amenities:** 3 restaurants; deli; lobby bar and pool bar; expansive outdoor pool; indoor pool; full-service spa; 3 whirlpools; sauna; steam room; access to Kids' Club at Marriott Casa Magna; concierge; travel agency; car rental; business center; shopping arcade; gift shop; salon; room service; laundry service; club floor w/special amenities and complimentary cocktails; medical services. *In room:* A/C, flatscreen TV, Wi-Fi, minibar, hair dryer, iron, safe.

Le Méridien Cancún Resort & Spa 𝄢𝄢

Le Méridien is among the most inviting of Cancún's luxury options, with a refined yet welcoming sense of personal service. From the intimate lobby and reception area to the best concierge service in Cancún, guests feel immediately pampered. The relatively small establishment is more elegant boutique hotel than immense resort—a welcome relief. The decor throughout the rooms and common areas is classy and comforting, not overdone. Rooms are generous in size with small balconies overlooking the pool; due to the hotel's design, rooms do not have ocean views. Each has a large marble bathroom with a separate tub and glassed-in shower. The hotel attracts many Europeans as well as younger, sophisticated travelers, and it is ideal for a second honeymoon.

A highlight of—or even a reason for—staying here is the **Spa del Mar,** one of Mexico's most complete European spa facilities, with more than 4,570 sq. m (49,190 sq. ft.) of services dedicated to your body and soul. A complete fitness center with extensive cardio and weight machines is on the upper level. The spa consists of a health snack bar, a full-service salon, and 14 treatment rooms, as well as men's and women's steam rooms, saunas, whirlpools, cold plunge pool, inhalation rooms, tranquillity rooms, lockers, and changing areas.

Aioli is a splendid fine-dining value (see "Where to Dine," later in this chapter).

Retorno del Rey Km 14, Zona Hotelera, 77500 Cancún, Q. Roo. ℰ **800/543-4300** in the U.S., or 998/881-2200. Fax 998/881-2201. www.meridiencancun.com.mx. 213 units. High season $593 (£326) double, $680 (£374) suite; low season $340 (£187) double, $470 (£259) suite. Ask about special spa packages. AE, DC, MC, V. Small pets accepted with prior reservation. **Amenities:** 2 restaurants; lobby bar; 3 cascading outdoor pools; 2 lighted championship tennis courts; whirlpool; watersports equipment/rentals; supervised children's program w/clubhouse, play equipment, wading pool; concierge; tour desk; car rental; business center; small shopping arcade; room service; massage *palapa* on the beach; babysitting; laundry service. *In room:* A/C, TV, minibar, hair dryer, iron, safe.

Ritz-Carlton Cancún ☆☆☆ *Kids*   The Ritz-Carlton's $15-million, post-Wilma restoration shows off this luxurious hotel to spectacular effect. The hotel fronts a (mostly) recovered 366m (1,200-ft.) white-sand beach, and all rooms overlook the ocean and pools. Several new features will enhance your stay, including: a culinary center that schedules not just daily Mexican and Mayan cooking classes, but wine and tequila tastings as well; and a group of specially designed "Itzy Bitzy Ritz Kids" guest rooms that offer cribs, changing tables, and the option of ordering formula, diapers, and other essentials before your arrival. Rooms and public areas have the low-key elegance that's a hallmark of the Ritz chain—think plush carpets, chandeliers, and fresh flowers, and rooms with marble bathrooms, fluffy featherbeds, and 400-count bed linens. The beachfront Kayantá Spa bases many of its treatments on traditional Maya rituals and therapies. The hotel's newest restaurant, **Casitas,** is the only oceanside dining spot in Cancún, where you can dine on steakhouse fare. in one of 16 candlelit cabañas. The hotel's primary restaurant, **Club Grill,** is reviewed in the "Where to Dine" section, later in this chapter.

Retorno del Rey 36, off Bulevar Kukulkán Km 13.5, 77500 Cancún, Q. Roo. ⓒ **800/241-3333** in the U.S. and Canada, or 998/881-0808. Fax 998/881-0815. www.ritz carlton.com. 365 units. Apr 10–Dec 20 $279–$569 (£155–£316) double, $439–$899 (£244–£499) club floor and suites; Dec 21–Apr 9 $459–$989 (£255–£549) double, $679–$1,329 (£377–£738) club floor and suites. Ask about golf, spa, and weekend packages. AE, MC, V. **Amenities:** 5 restaurants; lounge w/*ceviche* bar; 2 outdoor pools (heated in winter); 3 lighted tennis courts; fully equipped fitness center; Kayantá Spa; Kids Camp program; concierge; travel agency; business center; shopping arcade; salon; room service; babysitting; laundry service; dry cleaning; club floors; culinary center. *In room:* A/C, TV, minibar, hair dryer, iron, safe.

Riu Palace Las Américas ☆   The all-inclusive Riu Palace is part of a family of Riu resorts in Cancún known for their grand, opulent style. This one is the smallest of the three, and the most over-the-top, steeped in pearl-white Greco style. The location is prime—near the central shopping, dining, and nightlife centers, just 5 minutes walking to the Convention Center. All rooms are spacious junior suites with ocean or lagoon views, a separate seating area, and a balcony or terrace. Eight also feature a Jacuzzi. Two beautiful central pools overlook the ocean and a wide stretch of beach, with one heated during winter months. The hotel offers guests virtually 24 hours of all-inclusive snacks, meals, and beverages. And, if that's not enough, guests have exchange privileges at the Riu Cancún, next door. The hotel's European opulence stands in contrast to the mostly informal North American guests.

Bulevar Kukulkán, Lote 4, 77500 Cancún, Q. Roo. ① **888/666-8816** in the U.S., or 998/891-4300. www.riu.com. 372 units. High season $390–$790 (£215–£435) double; low season $337–$530 (£185–£292) double. Rates are all-inclusive. AE, MC, V. **Amenities:** 6 restaurants; 5 bars; 2 outdoor pools; access to golf and tennis; fitness center; spa (extra charges apply); sports program; nonmotorized watersports; room service; solarium. *In room:* A/C, TV, hair dryer, iron, safe.

Royal 𝒶𝒶   Opened in early 2007, this adults-only luxury hotel sits at the pinnacle of Cancún's all-inclusive establishments, offering a level of services and amenities unmatched almost anywhere. From the stunning infinity pools and gorgeous beach to the gourmet restaurants and sophisticated spa, the owners have spared no expense making this Cancún's Bellagio equivalent. The elegant marble lobby looks out one side to the Caribbean and the other to the lagoon. All of the innovative suites feature flatscreen TVs with CD/DVD players, marble bathrooms with rain showers, two-person Jacuzzis, and oceanview balconies with hammocks. Swim-up master suites have private plunge pools facing the resort's pool and beach; guests in the top-category suites have access to BMW Mini Coopers. The Mayan-inspired oceanview spa includes a massage room, Jacuzzi, sauna, traditional *temazcal* steam bath, massage waterfall, and a state-of-the-art fitness center. Actually, the range of services is almost hard to believe, except that you will be paying top dollar for it. The all-inclusive package includes gourmet meals, premium drinks, and evening entertainment.

Bulevar Kukulkán Km 11.5, 77500 Cancún, Q. Roo. ① **800/760-0944** in the U.S., or 998/881-7340. www.realresorts.com.mx. 285 units. $446–$804 (£245–£442) double suite. AE, DC, MC, V. No children younger than 16. **Amenities:** 6 restaurants; 8 bars; expansive outdoor pool; tennis court; well-equipped fitness center; full-service-spa; sauna; steam room; concierge; travel agency; car rental; business center; salon; room service; laundry service; club floor w/special amenities and complimentary cocktails. *In room:* A/C, flatscreen TV, Wi-Fi, minibar, hair dryer, iron, safe.

EXPENSIVE

Dreams Cancún Resort & Spa 𝒶 *Kids*   Formerly the Camino Real Cancún, the all-inclusive Dreams Resort is among the island's most appealing places to stay, located on 1.5 hectares (3¾ acres) at the tip of Punta Cancún. The setting is casual, and the hotel welcomes children. The architecture of Dreams is contemporary and sleek, with bright colors and strategic angles. Rooms in the newer 17-story club section have extra services and amenities. The lower-priced rooms offer lagoon views. The all-inclusive concept here includes gourmet meals, 24-hour room service, and premium brand drinks, as well as the use of all resort amenities, nonmotorized watersports, theme-night entertainment, and tips. The fitness center and spa are excellent.

Bulevar Kukulkán, 77500 Punta Cancún (Apdo. Postal 14), Cancún, Q. Roo. © 866/237-3267 in the U.S., or 998/848-7000. Fax 998/848-7001. www.dreamscancun.com. 379 units. High season $500 (£275) double, $560 (£308) club double; low season $370 (£204) double, $430 (£237) club double. AE, DC, MC, V. **Amenities:** 4 restaurants; nightclub; 2 outdoor pools; 2 lighted tennis courts; fitness center w/steam bath; watersports; kayaks; paddleboats; Kids' Club; travel agency; car rental; business center; salon; room service; massage; babysitting (w/advance notice); private saltwater lagoon w/dolphins and tropical fish; beach volleyball. *In room:* A/C, TV, minibar, hair dryer, iron, safe.

Marriott Casa Magna 𝔊𝔊 *Kids*   This sprawling Marriott resort is one of the most enticing family destinations in Cancún. Entering through a half-circle of Roman columns, you pass through a domed foyer to a wide, lavishly marbled lobby filled with plants and shallow pools. It looks out to the sparkling pool and Jacuzzi at the edge of the beach. Guest rooms are decorated with Mexican-Caribbean furnishings and tiled floors; most have oceanview balconies. The hotel caters to family travelers with specially priced packages (up to two children stay free with parent) and the Kids' Club Amigos supervised children's program. Among the many places to dine here, the *teppanyaki*-style (cook-at-your-table) Mikado Japanese restaurant is the best.

Bulevar Kukulkán Km 14.5, 77500 Cancún, Q. Roo © 800/228-9290 in the U.S., or 998/881-2000. Fax 998/881-2085. www.marriott.com. 452 units. $249–$309 (£137–£170) double; $454 (£250) and up suite. Ask about packages. AE, MC, V. **Amenities:** 6 restaurants; lobby bar w/live music; outdoor pool; 2 lighted tennis courts; health club w/saunas, whirlpool, aerobics, and juice bar; concierge; business center; travel agency; car rental; spa; salon w/massage and facials; room service; babysitting; laundry service. *In room:* A/C, TV, minibar, coffeemaker, hair dryer, iron, safe.

ME 𝔊   This latest opening of the Spanish ME hotel by Meliá brings to Cancún a new level of minimalist chic. Bathed in hues of beige and mauve, with polished marble, onyx lamps, and modern artwork, the hotel creates its own fashion statement—and the hip clientele reflects it. The modern lobby feels a bit like an upscale cocktail lounge, with trendy bars, sensual artwork, and chill-out music filling the space. Guest rooms have distinctive contemporary furnishings, plasma TVs, CD players, and marble bathrooms with rain showers and Aveda bath products; half look to the Caribbean Sea and the other half to the lagoon. The super-stylish Yhi Spa overlooks the ocean and offers body glows and exfoliations, aromatherapy massages, body masks, and wraps—this is a place to indulge yourself until you're entirely rejuvenated.

Bulevar Kukulkán Km 12, 77500 Cancún, Q. Roo. © 866/436-3542 in the U.S., or 998/881-2500. Fax 998/881-2502. www.mebymelia.com. 448 units. $357 (£196) and up double. AE, MC, V. **Amenities:** 3 restaurants; Internet cafe; 2 bars; 3 outdoor pools; beach club; fitness center; full-service luxury spa; whirlpool; salon; concierge; boutique; art gallery; concierge floor. *In room:* A/C, plasma TV, wireless Internet, minibar, hair dryer, safe.

The Westin Resort & Spa Cancún

The strikingly austere architecture of The Westin Resort, impressive with its elegant use of stone and marble, is the stamp of leading Latin American architect Ricardo Legorreta. The hotel consists of two sections, the main building and the more exclusive six-story Royal Beach Club. Guest rooms offer contemporary white furnishings and, while spacious, can feel a bit cold. Those on the sixth floor have balconies, and first-floor rooms include terraces. Rooms in the tower boast ocean or lagoon views, furniture with Olinalá lacquer accents, Berber area rugs, oak tables and chairs, and terraces with lounge chairs. It's important to note that this hotel is a 15- to 20-minute ride from the liveliest section of the hotel zone, making it a preferred choice for those who want a little more seclusion than Cancún typically offers. However, it's easy to join the action—buses stop in front, and taxis are readily available. The Westin renovated after Hurricane Wilma damaged the resort.

Bulevar Kukulkán Km 20, 77500 Cancún, Q. Roo. © 800/228-3000 in the U.S., 01-800/215-7000 in Mexico, or 998/848-7400. Fax 998/885-0666. www.starwood hotels.com/westin. 379 units. High season $319–$499 (£175–£274) double; low season $139–$299 (£76–£164) double. AE, DC, MC, V. **Amenities:** 3 restaurants; 2 bars; 8 outdoor pools; 2 lighted tennis courts; gym w/Stairmaster, bicycle, weights, and aerobics; sauna; *temazcal* (sweat lodge); concierge; travel agency; car rental; pharmacy/gift shop; salon; room service; massage; babysitting; laundry service. *In room:* A/C, TV, Wi-Fi, minibar, coffeemaker, hair dryer, iron, safe.

MODERATE

Blue Bay Getaway & Spa Cancún 𝓡

This adults-only getaway is a spirited, sexy all-inclusive resort favored by people looking for significant social interaction. By day, pool time is all about flirting, seducing, and getting a little wacky with adult games. Come night, theme dinners, shows, and other live entertainment keep the party going. Note that clothing is optional on the beaches of Blue Bay, which boasts calm waters for swimming. The comfortable, modern rooms are housed in two sections with lagoon, garden, or ocean views. Surrounded by acres of tropical gardens, this moderate hotel is ideally located at the northern end of the Hotel Zone, close to the major shopping plazas, restaurants, and nightlife.

Bulevar Kukulkán Km 3.5, 77500 Cancún, Q. Roo. (C) **800/211-1000** in the U.S., or 998/848-7900. Fax 998/848-7994. www.bluebaycancun.com. 385 units. High season $286–$325 (£157–£179) double; low season $225–$260 (£124–£143) double. Rates include food, beverages, and activities. AE, MC, V. Guests must be at least 21 years old. **Amenities:** 5 restaurants; 5 bars; 3 outdoor pools; 4 whirlpools; exercise room w/daily aerobics classes; nonmotorized watersports equipment; snorkeling and scuba lessons; marina; bikes; game room w/pool and Ping-Pong tables. *In room:* A/C, TV, hair dryer.

Flamingo Cancún *(Kids)*   The all-inclusive Flamingo seems to have been inspired by the dramatic, slope-sided architecture of the Dreams Cancún, but the Flamingo is considerably smaller and less expensive (guests have the option of opting out of the all-inclusive package, which includes three meals and domestic drinks). With two pools and a casual vibe, it's also a friendly, accommodating choice for families. The brightly colored blue and yellow guest rooms—all with balconies—border a courtyard facing the interior swimming pool and *palapa* pool-bar. The Flamingo lies in the heart of the island hotel district, opposite the Flamingo Shopping Center and close to other hotels, shopping centers, and restaurants.

Bulevar Kukulkán Km 11.5, 77500 Cancún, Q. Roo. (C) **998/848-8870.** Fax 998/ 883-1029. www.flamingocancun.com. 221 units. High season $190 (£105) double, low season $150 (£83) double; all-inclusive plan high season $280 (£154) double, low season $240 (£132) double. AE, MC, V. **Amenities:** 2 restaurants; 2 bars; 2 pools; fitness center; kids' club; travel agency; room service; safe. *In room:* A/C, TV, hair dryer, minibar.

Oasis Viva Beach Cancún   From the street, this all-inclusive hotel may not be much to look at, but on the ocean side you'll find a small but pretty patio garden and Cancún's best beach for safe swimming. The location is ideal, close to all the shops and restaurants near Punta Cancún and the Cancún Center. Rooms overlook the lagoon or the ocean, and all were remodeled post–Hurricane Wilma. They are large, with simple decor, marble floors, and either two double beds or a king-size bed. Several studios have kitchenettes. There is wheelchair access within the hotel's public areas.

Bulevar Kukulkán Km 8.5, 77500 Cancún, Q. Roo. (C) **800/221-2222** in the U.S., or 998/883-0800. Fax 998/883-2087. 216 units. High season $316 (£174) double; low season $185–$200 (£102–£110) double. Rates are all-inclusive. Discounted rate for children. AE, MC, V. **Amenities:** 4 restaurants; 5 bars; 2 outdoor pools (1 for adults, 1 for children); marina. *In room:* A/C, TV.

CANCUN CITY
MODERATE

Hotel Margaritas   Located in downtown Cancún, this four-story hotel (with elevator) is comfortable and unpretentious. The pleasantly decorated rooms, with white-tile floors and small balconies, are exceptionally clean and bright. Lounge chairs surround the small courtyard, which has a wading pool for children. The hotel offers complimentary safes at the front desk.

Av. Yaxchilán 41, SM22, Centro, 77500 Cancún, Q. Roo. © **01-800/640-7473** in Mexico, or 998/881-7870. Fax 998/884-1324. www.margaritascancun.com. 100 units. High season $112 (£62) double; low season $90 (£50) double. AE, MC, V. **Amenities:** Restaurant; outdoor pool; travel agency; room service; babysitting; Internet; billiards; currency exchange. *In room:* A/C, TV.

Radisson Hacienda Cancún ✦ *Value*   This is the top hotel in downtown Cancún, and one of the best values in the area. The Radisson offers all the expected comforts of a chain, yet in an atmosphere of Mexican hospitality. Resembling a hacienda, the business-friendly hotel has rooms that are set off from a large rotunda-style lobby, lush gardens, and a pleasant pool area. All have brightly colored fabric accents; views of the garden, the pool, or the street; and a small sitting area and balcony. Guests have access to shuttle service to Isla Cancún's beaches. The hotel lies within walking distance of downtown Cancún dining and shopping.

Av. Nader 1, SM2, Centro, 77500 Cancún, Q. Roo. © **800/333-3333** in the U.S., or 998/881-6500. Fax 998/884-7954. www.radissoncancun.com. 248 units. $140 (£77) double; $168 (£92) junior suite. AE, MC, V. **Amenities:** 2 restaurants; lively lobby bar; outdoor pool w/adjoining bar and separate wading area for children; lighted tennis courts; small gym; sauna; travel agency; car rental; salon. *In room:* A/C, TV, coffeemaker, hair dryer, iron, safe.

Rey del Caribe Hotel ✦✦ *Finds*   This ecological hotel is a unique oasis where every detail has been thought out to achieve the goal of creating environmentally friendly accommodations. You might easily forget you're in the midst of downtown Cancún in the tropical garden setting, with blooming orchids and other flowering plants. The lovely grounds include statues of Maya deities, hammocks, and a tiled swimming pool. There's a regularly changing schedule of yoga, Tai Chi, and meditation sessions, as well as special classes on astrology, tarot, and other subjects. The on-site spa offers facial and body treatments. Rooms are large and sunny, with your choice of one king-size or two full-size beds and terrace. The detail of ecological sensitivity is truly impressive, ranging from the use of collected rainwater to waste composting. Recycling is encouraged, and solar power is used wherever possible.

Av. Uxmal SM 2A (corner of Nader), 77500 Cancún, Q. Roo. ✆ 998/884-2028. Fax 988/884-9857. www.reycaribe.com. 31 units. High season $82 (£45) double; low season $55 (£30) double. Rates include breakfast. MC, V. **Amenities:** Outdoor pool; spa; massages; classes. *In room:* A/C, kitchenette.

INEXPENSIVE

Hotel Hacienda *(Value)*   This simple little hotel is a great value. The facade has been remodeled to look like a hacienda. Guest rooms are very basic; all have dark wood furnishings, whitewashed walls, small tiled bathrooms, and two double beds—but no views. There's a nice small pool and cafe under a shaded *palapa* in the back. You can easily walk to anywhere in downtown from here.

Sunyaxchen 39–40, 77500 Cancún, Q. Roo. ✆ 998/884-3672. Fax 998/884-1208. www.berny.com.mx. 36 units. High season $50 (£28) double; low season $45 (£25) double. Street parking. From Av. Yaxchilán, turn west on Sunyaxchen; it's on the right next to the Hotel Caribe International, opposite 100% Natural. **Amenities:** Outdoor pool. *In room:* A/C, TV, safe.

Refugio del Pirata Morgan *(Finds)*   Although not actually in the town of Cancún, but on the highway leading north from Cancún to Punta Sam, this is the place for those who want a simple and secluded beach vacation. A pirate's flag greets you at the entrance, and an international kite-surfing school is located on the premises. This ecological hotel lies on a wide, virgin stretch of beach, away from the crowd of hotels and nightlife; there are no phones or television, just blissful peace and quiet. Ten simple cabañas named for the predominate color of the decor feature *palapa* roofs, beds, and hammocks. A small restaurant offers a basic selection celebrating fresh fish—otherwise, the nearest restaurant is 2km (1¼ miles) away.

Carretera Punta Sam, Isla Blanca, Km 9, 77500 Cancún, Q. Roo. ✆ 998/860-3386 (within Mexico dial 044 first, as this is a cellphone). 10 units. $50 (£28) room; $5 (£2.75) hammock. Camping available $6 (£3.30) adult, $3 (£1.65) children. No credit cards. **Amenities:** Restaurant; kite-surfing school; kayaks and snorkeling equipment for rent. *In room:* Fan, no phone.

Xbalamqué   Creatively designed to resemble a Maya temple, this downtown hotel features a full-service spa, lovely pool and waterfall, and an authentic Mexican cantina. Live music plays evenings in the bookstore/cafe adjacent to the lobby. Guest rooms have rustic furnishings with regional touches, colorful tile work, and small bathrooms with showers. Ask for a room overlooking the ivy-filled courtyard. A tour desk is available to help you plan your vacation activities, and the spa offers some of the best rates of any hotel in Cancún.

Av. Yaxchilán 31, Sm. 22, Mza. 18, 77500 Cancún, Q. Roo. © **998/884-9690**. Fax 998/ 884-9690. www.xbalamque.com. 108 units. High season $95 (£52) double; low season $75 (£41) double. AE, MC, V. **Amenities:** Restaurant; cantina; cafe; outdoor pool; spa; travel agency. *In room:* A/C, TV.

2 Where to Dine

U.S.-based franchise chains, which really need no introduction, dominate the Cancún restaurant scene. These include Hard Rock Cafe, Rainforest Cafe, Tony Roma's, T.G.I. Friday's, Ruth's Chris Steak House, and the gamut of fast-food burger places. The establishments listed here are locally owned, one-of-a-kind restaurants or exceptional selections at area hotels. Many schedule live music. Unless otherwise indicated, parking is free.

One unique way to combine dinner with sightseeing is aboard the **Lobster Dinner Cruise** (© **998/849-4748**). Cruising around the tranquil, turquoise waters of the lagoon, passengers feast on lobster dinners accompanied by wine. Cost is $79 per person. There are two daily departures from the Aquatours Marina (Bulevar Kukulkán 6.5). A sunset cruise leaves at 5pm during the winter and 5:30pm during the summer; a moonlight cruise leaves at 8pm winter, 8:30pm summer. Another—albeit livelier—lobster dinner option is the **Captain Hook Lobster Dinner Cruise** (© **998/849-4451**), which is similar, but with the added attraction of a pirate show, making this the choice for families. It costs $83 (£46) per person, departs at 7pm from El Embarcadero, and returns at 10:30pm.

CANCUN ISLAND
VERY EXPENSIVE

Aioli 🏵🏵 FRENCH   The quality and originality of the cuisine and excellence of service make this a top choice for fine-dining in Cancún. The Provençal—but definitely not provincial—Aioli offers exquisite French and Mediterranean gourmet specialties in a warm and cozy country French setting. Though it serves perhaps the best breakfast buffet in Cancún (for $24/£13), most diners from outside the hotel come here in the evening, when low lighting and superb service promise a romantic experience. Delectable starters include foie gras and risotto with wild mushrooms; among the best main courses are pan-seared sea scallops, roasted lamb with a tarragon crust, and breast of duck. Desserts are decadent, especially the signature "Fifth Element," rich with chocolate.

In Le Méridien Cancún Resort & Spa, Retorno del Rey Km 14. ⓒ **998/881-2200.** Reservations recommended. Main courses $24–$37 (£13–£20). AE, MC, V. Daily 6:30am–11pm.

Club Grill ⟳⟳⟳ INTERNATIONAL   This is the place for that special night out. Cancún's most elegant and stylish restaurant is also among its most delicious. Even rival restaurateurs give it envious thumbs up. The gracious service starts as you enter the anteroom, with its comfortable seating and selection of fine drinks. It continues in a candlelit dining room with shimmering silver and crystal. Elegant plates of peppered scallops, truffles, and potatoes in tequila sauce; grilled lamb; or mixed grill arrive at a leisurely pace. The restaurant has smoking and nonsmoking sections. A band plays romantic music for dancing from 8pm on.

In the Ritz-Carlton Cancún, Retorno del Rey, 36 Bulevar Kukulkán Km 13.5. ⓒ **998/881-0808.** Reservations required. No sandals or tennis shoes; men must wear long pants. Main courses $11–$40 (£6.05–£22). AE, DC, MC, V. Tues–Sun 7–11pm.

Lorenzillo's ⟳⟳⟳ (Kids) SEAFOOD   Live lobster is the overwhelming favorite, and part of the appeal is selecting your dinner out of the giant lobster tank set in the lagoon (Lorenzillo's sits right on the lagoon under a giant *palapa* roof). A dock leads down to the main dining area, and when that's packed (which is often), a wharf-side bar handles the overflow. In addition to lobster—which comes grilled, steamed, or stuffed—good bets are shrimp stuffed with cheese and wrapped in bacon, the *pescador* (Caribbean grouper prepared to taste), and seafood-stuffed calamari. Desserts include the tempting "Martinique": warm apples, raisins, and walnuts caramelized with rum and wrapped in a pastry with vanilla ice cream. The sunset pier offers a lighter menu of cold seafood, sandwiches, and salads. There's a festive, friendly atmosphere, and children are very welcome—after all, most of the patrons are wearing bibs!

Bulevar Kukulkán Km 10.5. ⓒ **998/883-1254.** www.lorenzillos.com.mx. Reservations recommended. Main courses $19–$44 (£10–£24). AE, MC, V. Daily 1pm–12:30am.

EXPENSIVE

Casa de las Margaritas ⟳ MEXICAN   La Casa de las Margaritas is a celebration of the flavors and *¡fiesta!* spirit of Mexico. With a decor as vibrant as a *piñata,* and a soundtrack of background music that ranges from mariachi to *marimba,* the experience here is a crash course in the festive spirit of this colorful country. On the menu, best bets include the Margarita shrimp, sautéed in garlic, cream, and chipotle chile sauce; chicken breast served with three flavorful mole sauces; or the platter of chicken enchiladas topped with tomato-and-sun-dried-pepper sauce. Located inside La Isla shopping center, Casa de las Margaritas also serves a spectacular Sunday brunch. Live music is offered nightly.

Paseo Kukulkán Km 12.5, La Isla Shopping Mall, Loc. E-17. (C) **998/883-3222** or -3054. www.lacasadelasmargaritas.com. Reservations recommended. Main courses $6–$38 (£3.30–£21). AE, MC, V. Mon–Sat 11am–midnight; Sun brunch noon–5pm.

Casa Rolandi 𝕽𝕽 SWISS/ITALIAN   Like its sister location in Isla Mujeres, Casa Rolandi blends sophisticated Swiss-Italian cuisine with fresh Caribbean fish and Mexican produce. Famous personalities, from international actors to American presidents, have dined here. The casually elegant restaurant offers white linen tables and candles at night, but welcomes informal dress. Among the creative selections are homemade ravioli stuffed with wild mushrooms over a creamy Alba truffle sauce, taglioni with sautéed shrimp and ginger sprinkled with white wine, and fresh fish (usually snapper or sea bass) baked in salt and accompanied by fresh vegetables and seasoned mashed potatoes. Finish with the sublime tiramisu served with chocolate and rum cream. Service is personalized and friendly.

Bulevar Kukulkán Km 8.5, in Plaza Caracol. (C) **998/883-2557.** Reservations recommended. Main courses $15–$35 (£8.25–£19). AE, MC, V. Sun–Thurs 1–11:30pm; Fri–Sat 1pm–2am.

Gustino 𝕽𝕽 ITALIAN   JW Marriott's signature restaurant Gustino offers romantic Italian dining unsurpassed in Cancún. The refined dining room includes a gorgeous centerpiece candle display, floor-to-ceiling windows looking out to a lazy man-made lagoon and the beach beyond, and live saxophone. Among the rich selection of *antipasti,* the black shell mussels, minestrone, and *Festival dei Frutti de Mare* for two are the best. For a main course, consider homemade pasta, the veal scaloppine, or filet of beef tenderloin in a red-wine sauce served with fresh vegetables. There's also a wide selection of fresh fish and seafood. Gustino boasts an open kitchen and wine cellar with an excellent variety of international grapes. Service is outstanding.

In the JW Marriott, Bulevar Kukulkán Km 14.5. (C) **998/848-9600.** Reservations required. Main courses $14–$27 (£7.70–£15). AE, DC, MC, V. Daily 6–11pm.

Laguna Grill ✿✿ FUSION   Laguna Grill offers diners a contemporary culinary experience in a picturesque setting overlooking the lagoon. A tropical garden welcomes you at the entrance, while a small creek traverses the restaurant set with tables made from the trunks of tropical trees. As magical as the decor is, the real star here is the kitchen, with its selection of Pacific Rim cuisine fused with regional flavors. Starters include martini *gyoza* (steamed dumplings), filled with shrimp and vegetables, or seafood *ceviche* in sesame oil and curry. Fish and seafood dominate the menu, in preparations that combine Asian and Mexican flavors such as ginger, cilantro, garlic, and hoisin sauce. Grilled shrimp are marinated in rum, mint, and lime; surf and turf fusion dishes may include grilled lobster, beef, and shrimp skewers. For beef-lovers, the rib-eye served over garlic, spinach, and sweet-potato mash is sublime. Desserts are as creative as the main dishes; the pineapple-papaya strudel in Malibu rum sauce stands out. If you're an early diner, request a table on the outside deck for a spectacular sunset view. An impressive selection of wines is available.

Bulevar Kukulkán Km 16.5. © **998/885-0267.** www.lagunagrill.com.mx. Reservations recommended. Main courses $11–$34 (£6.05–£19). AE, MC, V. Daily 2pm–midnight.

Paloma Bonita ✿ (Kids) REGIONAL/MEXICAN/NOUVELLE MEXICAN   In a stylish setting overlooking the water, Paloma Bonita captures the essence of Mexico through its music and food. Since Paloma Bonita lies in a hotel (Dreams Cancún), prices are higher than at traditional Mexican restaurants in Ciudad Cancún, but this is a good choice for the Hotel Zone. There are three sections: La Cantina Jalisco, with an open kitchen and tequila bar; the Salón Michoacán, which features that state's cuisine; and the Patio Oaxaca. The menu encompasses the best of Mexico's other cuisines, with a few international dishes. Prix-fixe dinners include appetizer, main course, and dessert. Jazz trios, *marimba* and *Jarocha* music, and mariachis serenade you while you dine. A nice starter is Mitla salad, with slices of the renowned Oaxaca cheese dribbled with olive oil and coriander dressing. Wonderful stuffed chile La Doña—a mildly hot poblano pepper filled with lobster and *huitlacoche* (a type of mushroom that grows on corn) in a cream sauce—comes as an appetizer or a main course.

In the Hotel Dreams, Punta Cancún (enter from the street). © **998/848-7000,** ext. 7965. Reservations recommended. Prix-fixe dinner $30–$45 (£17–£25); main courses $25–$35(£14–£19). AE, DC, MC, V. Daily 6:30–11:30pm.

Puerto Madero *&& ARGENTINE/STEAKS/SEAFOOD* As a tribute to the famed Puerto Madero of Buenos Aires, this restaurant has quickly earned a reputation for its authentic Argentine cuisine and ambience. Overlooking the Nichupté Lagoon, the decor re-creates a 20th-century dock warehouse, with elegant touches of modern architecture. Puerto Madero offers an extensive selection of prime quality beef cuts, pastas, grilled fish, and shellfish, meticulously prepared with Buenos Aires gusto. In addition to the classic *carpaccio,* the tuna tartar and halibut steak are favorites, but the real standouts here are the tender grilled steaks (particularly the rib-eye), served in ample portions. Enjoy a cocktail or glass of wine from the extensive selection, while viewing the sunset from the lagoon-side deck. Service is excellent.

Marina Barracuda, Bulevar Kukulkán Km 14. (*) 998/885-2829 or -2830. www. puertomaderocancun.com. Reservations recommended. Main courses $14–$52 (£7.70–£29). AE, MC, V. Daily 1pm–1am.

MODERATE

La Destilería MEXICAN To experience Mexico's favorite export on an enticing terrace overlooking the lagoon, this is your place (keep an eye out for Tequila, the lagoon crocodile who often comes to visit). La Destilería is more than a tequila-inspired restaurant; it's a minimuseum honoring the "spirit" of Mexico. It serves over 150 brands of tequila, including some treasures that never find their way across the country's northern border. No surprise, the margaritas are among the best on the island. When you decide to order some food with your tequila, you'll find an authentic Mexican menu, with everything from quesadillas with squash blossom flowers, to shrimp in a delicate tequila-lime sauce. There are even *escamoles* (crisp-fried ant eggs) as an appetizer for the adventurous—or for those whose squeamishness has been diminished by the tequila!

Bulevar Kukulkán Km 12.65, across from Kukulcán Plaza. (*) 998/885-1086 or -1087. www.cmr.ws. Main courses $12–$28. AE, MC, V. Daily 1pm–midnight.

La Fisheria *& (Kids SEAFOOD* Seafood lovers will find heavenly bliss at this casual yet inviting restaurant overlooking Bulevar Kukulkán and the lagoon. The expansive menu includes shrimp bisque, seafood salad, and *ceviche* tostadas. For a main course, consider the calamari steak with shrimp, seafood paella, surf and turf, or fresh fish prepared any way you want, including the specialty grouper filet stuffed with seafood in lobster sauce. The menu changes daily, but there's always *tikin xik,* that great Yucatecan grilled fish marinated in *achiote* (a spice) sauce. For those not inclined toward seafood, a pizza from the wood-burning oven, or perhaps a grilled chicken or beef dish, might do. La Fisheria has a nonsmoking section.

Plaza Caracol shopping center, Bulevar Kukulkán Km 8.5, 2nd floor. ℭ 998/883-1395. Main courses $9–$33 (£4.95–£18). AE, MC, V. Daily 11am–11pm.

Thai ☆☆☆ *Moments* THAI This feels a lot more like Thailand than the edge of a Mexican shopping plaza. With a backdrop that includes three dolphins cavorting in an enormous aquarium, Thai restaurant offers a unique and calming setting with individual *palapas* (each with its own table and sofa) built over the expansive lagoon. Unobtrusive service, soft red and blue lighting, and Asian chill and lounge music contribute to the romantic ambience. Such classic Thai specialties as spicy chicken soup, Thai salad, chicken satay, and chicken and shrimp curries are served in an ultrachic atmosphere. A DJ works the bar on weekends. The restaurant opens at sunset.

La Isla Shopping Center, Loc. B-4. ℭ 998/144-0364. Reservations recommended during high season. Main courses $7.50–$28 (£4.15–£15). AE, MC, V. Daily 6pm–1am.

CANCUN CITY
EXPENSIVE

La Habichuela ☆☆☆ *Moments* GOURMET SEAFOOD In a musically accented garden setting with flowering hibiscus trees, this downtown restaurant is ideal for a romantic evening. For an all-out culinary adventure, try *habichuela* (string bean) soup; shrimp in any number of sauces, including Jamaican tamarind, tequila, or ginger and mushroom; and Maya coffee with *xtabentun* (a strong, sweet, anise-based liqueur). Grilled seafood and steaks are excellent, and the menu includes luscious *ceviches,* Caribbean lobsters, an inventive seafood "parade," and shish kabob flambé. For something divine, try *cocobichuela,* lobster and shrimp in curry served in a coconut shell and topped with fruit. Top it off with one of the boozy butterscotch crepes. Service here is fabulous.

Margaritas 25. ℭ 998/884-3158. www.lahabichuela.com. Reservations recommended in high season. Main courses $13–$43 (£7.15–£24). AE, MC, V. Daily noon–midnight.

Périco's ☆☆ *Finds* MEXICAN/SEAFOOD/STEAKS Périco's is a joyous parade of performance, play, and brightly colored hilarity.

The unique restaurant features entertaining waiters dressed in a variety of festive costumes, murals that seem to dance off the walls, a bar area with saddles for barstools, and leather tables and chairs. Its extensive menu offers well-prepared steak, seafood, and traditional Mexican dishes for reasonable rates (except for lobster). This is a place not only to eat and drink, but also to let loose and join in the fun, so don't be surprised if diners drop their forks and don sombreros to shimmy and shake in a conga line around the dining room. The entertainment kicks off at 7:30pm.

Yaxchilán 61. ⓒ 998/884-3152. www.pericos.com.mx. Reservations recommended. Main courses $14–$39 (£7.70–£21). AE, MC, V. Daily noon–1am.

MODERATE

Labná *ⒻⒻ* YUCATECAN   To steep yourself in Yucatecan cuisine and music, head directly to this showcase of Maya moods and regional foods. Specialties served here include a sublime lime soup, *poc chuc* (marinated, barbecue-style pork), chicken or pork *pibil* (sweet and spicy barbecue sauce served over shredded meat), and appetizers such as *papadzules* (tortillas stuffed with boiled eggs in a pumpkin seed sauce). The Labná Special is a sampler of four typically Yucatecan main courses, including *poc chuc,* while another specialty of the house is baked suckling pig, served with guacamole. The refreshing Yucatecan beverage, *agua de chaya*—a blend of sweetened water and the leaf of the *chaya* plant, abundant in the area, to which sweet Xtabentun liquor (a type of anise) can be added for an extra kick—is also served here. The vaulted ceiling dining room is decorated with black-and-white photographs of the region dating from the 1900s. A local trio plays weekend afternoons.

Margaritas 29, next to City Hall and the Habichuela restaurant. ⓒ 998/892-3056. Main courses $7–$20 (£3.85–£11). AE, MC, V. Daily noon–10pm.

INEXPENSIVE

100% Natural *Ⓕ* VEGETARIAN/MEXICAN   If you want a healthy reprieve from an overindulgent night—or just like your meals as fresh and natural as possible—this is your oasis. No matter what your dining preference, you owe it to yourself to try a Mexican tradition, the fresh-fruit *licuado.* These smoothie-like drinks combine fresh fruit, ice, and water or milk. More creative combinations may mix in yogurt, granola, or other goodies. 100% Natural serves more than just meal-quality drinks—there's a bountiful selection of simple Mexican fare and terrific sandwiches served on whole-grain bread, with options for vegetarians. Breakfast is delightful and easy on the wallet. The space abounds with plants and cheery colors, and there's an attached bakery featuring all-natural baked goods. There are several 100% Natural locations in town, including branches at Playa Chac-Mool, across from Señor Frog's, and downtown.

Av. Sunyaxchen 63. © 998/884-0102. www.100natural.com.mx. Reservations not accepted. Main courses $5–$15 (£2.75–£8.25). MC, V. Daily 7am–11pm.

Pizza Rolandi ☆ *Kids* ITALIAN   This is an institution in Cancún, and the Rolandi name is synonymous with dining in both Cancún and neighboring Isla Mujeres. Pizza Rolandi and its branch in Isla Mujeres (see chapter 4) have become standards for dependably good casual fare. At this shaded outdoor patio restaurant, you can choose from almost two dozen delicious, if greasy, wood-oven pizzas and a full selection of spaghetti, calzones, Italian-style chicken and beef, and desserts.

Cobá 12. © **998/884-4047.** Fax 998/884-4047. www.rolandi.com. Pasta $8–$11 (£4.40–£6.05); pizza and main courses $7–$13 (£3.85–£7.15). AE, MC, V. Daily noon–11pm.

Roots INTERNATIONAL   This popular hangout for local residents is also a fun spot for visitors to Cancún. Located in the heart of downtown, this restaurant and jazz club offers a unique cosmopolitan ambience. The Caribbean-themed menu offers a range of casual dining choices, including salads, pastas, and even fresh squid. It's accompanied by live music, including reggae, flamenco, jazz, and fusion. Decking the walls are original works of art by local painters.

Tulipanes 26, SM 22. © **998/884-2437.** roots@Cancun.com. Main courses $6–$17 (£3.30–£9.35). MC, V. Tues–Sat 6pm–1am.

3

What to See & Do in Cancún

You will run out of vacation days before you run out of things to do in Cancún. Snorkeling, dolphin swims, jungle tours, and visits to ancient Maya ruins and modern ecological theme parks are among the most popular diversions. A dozen malls house name-brand and duty-free shops (with European goods at prices better than in the U.S.), and there are more than 350 restaurants and nightclubs.

In addition to having attractions of its own, Cancún is a convenient distance to the more traditional resorts of Isla Mujeres and the coastal zone now known as the Riviera Maya—extending down from Cancún, through Playa del Carmen, to the Maya ruins at Tulum, Cozumel, Chichén Itzá, and Cobá. All make for an easy day trip. See chapter 4 for Isla Mujeres and destinations along the Riviera Maya. Tulum, Chichén Itzá, and Cobá are discussed in chapter 5. For more on Cozumel, see *Frommer's Cancún, Cozumel & the Yucatán 2008.*

1 Beaches, Watersports & Boat Tours

BEACHES

Big hotels dominate the best stretches of beach. All of Mexico's beaches are public property, so you can use the beach of any hotel by walking through the lobby or directly onto the sand. Be especially careful on beaches fronting the open Caribbean, where the undertow can be quite strong. By contrast, the waters of Bahía de Mujeres (Mujeres Bay), at the north end of the island, are usually calm and ideal for swimming. Get to know Cancún's water-safety pennant system, and make sure to check the flag at any beach or hotel before entering the water. Here's how it goes:

White	Excellent
Green	Normal conditions (safe)
Yellow	Changeable, uncertain (use caution)
Black or **Red**	Unsafe—use the swimming pool instead!

In the Caribbean, storms can arrive and conditions can change from safe to unsafe in minutes, so be alert: If dark clouds are heading your way, make for the shore and wait until the storm passes.

Playa Tortuga (Turtle Beach), Playa Langosta (Lobster Beach), Playa Linda (Pretty Beach), and Playa Las Perlas (Beach of the Pearls) are some of the public beaches. At most beaches, you can rent a sailboard and take lessons, ride a parasail, or partake in a variety of watersports. There's a small but beautiful portion of public beach on **Playa Caracol,** by the Xcaret Terminal. It faces the calm waters of Bahía de Mujeres and, for that reason, is preferable to those facing the Caribbean.

WATERSPORTS

Many beachside hotels offer watersports concessions that rent rubber rafts, kayaks, and snorkeling equipment. On the calm Nichupté lagoon are outlets for renting **sailboats, jet skis, sailboards,** and **water skis.** Prices vary and are often negotiable, so check around.

DEEP-SEA FISHING

You can arrange a day of deep-sea fishing at one of the numerous piers or travel agencies for $220 to $360 (£121–£198) for 4 hours, $420 (£231) for 6 hours, and $520 (£286) for 8 hours for up to four people; for up to eight people, the prices are $420 (£231) for 4 hours, $550 (£303) for 6 hours, or $680 (£374) for 8 hours. Marinas will sometimes help assemble a group. Charters include a captain, a first mate, bait, gear, and beverages. Rates are lower if you depart from Isla Mujeres or from Cozumel—and frankly, the fishing is better closer to those departure points.

SCUBA & SNORKELING

Known for its shallow reefs, dazzling color, and diversity of life, Cancún is one of the best places in the world for beginning scuba diving. Punta Nizuc is the northern tip of the **Gran Arrecife Maya (Great Mesoamerican Reef),** the largest reef in the Western Hemisphere and one of the largest in the world. In addition to the sea life along this reef system, several sunken boats add a variety of dive options. Inland, a series of caverns and *cenotes* (wellsprings) are fascinating venues for the more experienced diver. Drift diving is the norm here, with popular dives going to the reefs at **El Garrafón** and the **Cave of the Sleeping Sharks**—although be aware that the famed "sleeping sharks" have departed, driven off by too many people watching them snooze.

A variety of hotels offer resort courses that teach the basics of diving—enough to make shallow dives and slowly ease your way into this underwater world of unimaginable beauty. One preferred dive operator is **Scuba Cancún,** Bulevar Kukulkán Km 5 (© **998/849-4736;**

www.scubacancun.com.mx), on the lagoon side. Full certification takes 3 days and costs $410 (£226). Scuba Cancún is open daily from 7am to 8pm, and accepts MasterCard and Visa. For certified divers, Scuba Cancún also offers diving trips in good weather to 18 nearby reefs, as well as to Cenotes Caverns (9m/30 ft.) and Cozumel. The average dive is around 11m (36 ft.), while advanced divers descend farther (up to 18m/60 ft.). Two-tank dives to reefs around Cancún cost $68 (£37); those to farther destinations cost $140 (£77). Discounts apply if you bring your own equipment. Dives usually start around 9:30am and return by 1:30pm. Snorkeling trips cost $27 (£15) and leave every afternoon at 1:30pm and 4pm for shallow reefs about a 20-minute boat ride away.

The largest dive operator is **Aquaworld,** across from the Meliá Cancún at Bulevar Kukulkán Km 15.2 (© **998/848-8327;** www.aquaworld.com.mx). It offers resort courses and diving from a man-made anchored dive platform, Paradise Island. Aquaworld has the **Sub See Explorer,** a boat with picture windows that hang beneath the surface. The boat doesn't submerge—it's an updated version of a glass-bottom boat—but it does provide nondivers with a look at life beneath the sea. This outfit is open 24 hours a day and accepts all major credit cards.

Besides snorkeling at **El Garrafón Natural Park** (see "Boating Excursions," below), travel agencies offer an all-day excursion to the natural wildlife habitat of **Isla Contoy,** which usually includes time for snorkeling. The island, 90 minutes past Isla Mujeres, is a major nesting area for birds and a treat for nature lovers. You can call any travel agent or see any hotel tour desk to get a selection of boat tours to Isla Contoy. Prices range from $45 to $70 (£25–£39), depending on the length of the trip, and generally include drinks and snorkeling equipment.

The Great Mesoamerican Reef also offers exceptional snorkeling opportunities. In Puerto Morelos, 37km (23 miles) south of Cancún, the reef hugs the coastline for 15km (9⅓ miles). The reef is so close to the shore (about 460m/1,509 ft.) that it forms a natural barrier for the village and keeps the waters calm on the inside of the reef. The water here is shallow, from 1.5 to 9m (5–30 ft.), resulting in ideal conditions for snorkeling. Stringent environmental regulations implemented by the local community have kept the reef here unspoiled. Only a select few companies are allowed to offer snorkel trips, and they must adhere to guidelines that will ensure the reef's preservation. **Cancún Mermaid** (© **998/843-6517;** www.cancunmermaid.com) is considered the best—it's a family-run ecotour company that has operated in the area since the 1970s. It's known for highly personalized service. The tour typically takes snorkelers to two sections of the reef, spending about an hour in each area. When conditions allow, the boat drops off snorkelers and then follows them along with the current—an activity known as "drift snorkeling," which enables snorkelers to see as much of the reef as possible. The trip costs $50 (£28) for adults, $35 (£19) for children, and includes boat, snorkeling gear, life jackets, a light lunch, bottled water, sodas, and beer, plus round-trip transportation to and from Puerto Morelos from Cancún hotels. Departures are Monday through Saturday at 9am. For snorkelers who just can't get enough, a combo tour for $30 (£17) more adds a bicycle tour to additional snorkeling destinations. Reservations are required at least 1 day in advance; MasterCard and Visa are accepted.

JET-SKI TOURS

Several companies offer the popular **Jungle Cruise,** which takes you by small boat or WaveRunner (you drive your own watercraft) through Cancún's lagoon and mangrove estuaries out into the Caribbean Sea and a shallow reef. The excursion runs about 2½ hours and costs $55 (£30), including snorkeling equipment and bottled water. Many people prefer the companies offering two-person boats rather than WaveRunners, since they can sit side by side rather than one behind the other.

The names of jet-ski operators offering excursions change often. To find out what's available, check with a local travel agent or hotel tour desk. The popular **Aquaworld,** Bulevar Kukulkán Km 15.2 (© **998/848-8327**), calls its trip the Jungle Tour and charges $55 (£30) for the 2½-hour excursion, which includes 45 minutes of snorkeling time. It even gives you a free snorkel, but has the less desirable one-behind-the-other seating configuration. Departures are daily every hour between 8am and 3pm.

BOATING EXCURSIONS
TO ISLA MUJERES

The island of **Isla Mujeres,** just 13km (8 miles) offshore, is one of the most pleasant day trips from Cancún. At one end is **El Garrafón Natural Park,** which is good for snorkeling. At the other end is a captivating village with small shops, restaurants, and hotels, and **Playa Norte,** the island's best beach. If you're looking for relaxation and can spare the time, it's worth several days. For complete information about the island, see chapter 4.

There are four ways to get there: **public ferry** from Puerto Juárez, which takes between 15 and 20 minutes; **shuttle boat** from Playa Linda or Playa Tortuga—an hour-long ride, with irregular service; **watertaxi** (more expensive, but faster), next to the Xcaret Terminal; and daylong **pleasure-boat trips,** most of which leave from the Playa Linda pier.

The inexpensive but fast Puerto Juárez **public ferries** ✦ lie just a few kilometers from downtown Cancún. From Cancún City, take the Ruta 8 bus on Avenida Tulum to Puerto Juárez. The air-conditioned *Caribbean Express* and *Ultramar* boats (15–20 min.) cost $4 (£2.20) per person. Departures are every half-hour from 6 to 8:30am and then every 15 minutes until 8:30pm. The slower *Caribbean Savage* (45–60 min.) costs about $3.50 (£1.95). It departs every 2 hours, or less frequently depending on demand. Upon arrival, the ferry docks in downtown Isla Mujeres near all the shops, restaurants, hotels, and Norte beach. You'll need a taxi to get to El Garrafón park at the other end of the island. You can stay as long as you like on the island and return by ferry, but be sure to confirm the time of the last returning ferry.

Pleasure-boat cruises to Isla Mujeres are a favorite pastime. Modern motor yachts, catamarans, trimarans, and even old-time sloops—more than 25 boats a day—take swimmers, sun lovers, snorkelers, and shoppers out on the translucent waters. Some tours include a snorkeling stop at El Garrafón, lunch on the beach, and a short time for shopping in downtown Isla Mujeres. Most leave at 9:30 or 10am, last about 5 or 6 hours, and include continental breakfast, lunch, and rental of snorkel gear. Others, particularly sunset and night cruises, go to beaches away from town for pseudo-pirate shows and include a lobster dinner or Mexican buffet. If you want to actually see Isla Mujeres, go on a morning cruise, or travel on your own using the public ferry from Puerto Juárez. Prices for the day cruises run around $45 (£25) per person.

TO EL GARRAFON

An all-inclusive entrance fee of $65 (£36) to **Garrafón Natural Reef Park** ✦✦ (© **998/849-4748;** www.garrafon.com) includes transportation from Cancún, meals, drinks, access to the reef and a museum, as well as use of snorkel gear, kayaks, inner tubes, life vests, the pool, hammocks, and public facilities and showers (but not towels, so bring your own). There are also nature trails and several on-site restaurants.

Tips **An All-Terrain Tour**

Cancún Mermaid (© **998/843-6517**; www.cancunmermaid.com) offers all-terrain-vehicle (ATV) jungle tours for $72 (£30) per person or $55 (£30) per person if riding double. The ATV tours travel through the jungles of Cancún and emerge on the beaches of the Riviera Maya. The 5-hour tour (including transportation time) includes equipment, instruction, the services of a tour guide, lunch, and bottled water; it departs daily at 8am, 10:30am, and 1:30pm. The company picks you up at the Plaza Kukulcán.

TO THE REEFS

Other excursions go to the **reefs** in glass-bottom boats, so you can have a near-scuba-diving experience and see many colorful fish. However, the reefs are some distance from the shore and are impossible to reach on windy days with choppy seas. They've also suffered from overvisitation, and their condition is far from pristine. Nautibus's **Atlantis Submarine** (© **987/872-5671;** www.atlantis adventures.com) takes you close to the aquatic action. Departures vary, depending on the weather. Prices are $79 (£43) for adults, $45 (£25) for children ages 4 to 12. The submarine descends to a depth of 30m (98 ft.). Atlantis Submarine departs Monday to Saturday every hour from 8am until 2pm; the tour lasts about an hour. The submarine departs from Cozumel, so you either need to take a ferry to get there or purchase the package that includes round-trip transportation from your hotel in Cancún ($103/£57 adults, $76/£42 children 4–12). Reservations are recommended.

2 Outdoor Activities & Attractions

OUTDOOR ACTIVITIES

DOLPHIN SWIMS

On Isla Mujeres, you have the opportunity to swim with dolphins at **Dolphin Discovery** ★★ (© **998/877-0207** or 849/4757; www. dolphindiscovery.com). Groups of eight people swim with two dolphins and one trainer. Swimmers view an educational video and spend time in the water with the trainer and the dolphins before enjoying 15 minutes of free swimming time with them. Reservations are recommended, and you must arrive an hour before your assigned swimming time, at 10:30am, noon, 2pm, or 3:30pm. The cost is

$139 (£76) per person for the Dolphin Royal Swim. There are less expensive programs that allow you to learn about, touch, and hold the dolphins (but not swim with them) starting at $79 (£43). Ferry transfers from Playa Langosta in Cancún are available.

La Isla Shopping Center, Bulevar Kukulkán Km 12.5, has an impressive **Interactive Aquarium** (© 998/883-0411; -0436, or -0413; www.aquariumcancun.com.mx), with dolphin swims and shows and the chance to feed a shark while immersed in the water in an acrylic cage. Open exhibition tanks enable visitors to touch a variety of marine life, including sea stars and manta rays. The educational dolphin program costs $65 (£36), while the dolphin swim is $135 (£74) and the shark-feeding experience runs $65 (£36). The entrance fee to the aquarium is $13 (£7.15) for adults, $9 (£4.95) for children, and it's open daily from 9am to 6pm.

For information on the ethics of swimming with dolphins, see p. 99.

GOLF & TENNIS

The 18-hole **Pok-Ta-Pok Club,** or Club de Golf Cancún (© **998/ 883-0871**), is a Robert Trent Jones, Sr., design on the northern leg of the island. Greens fees run $105 (£58) for 18 holes including golf cart (discounted twilight fees), with clubs renting for $40 (£22). A caddy costs $20 (£11). The club is open daily from 6:30am to 6:30pm, accepts American Express, MasterCard, and Visa, and has tennis courts.

The **Hilton Cancún Golf & Spa Resort** (© 998/881-8016) has a championship 18-hole, par-72 course around the Ruinas Del Rey. Greens fees for the public are typically $199 (£109) for 18 holes and $149 (£82) for 9 holes; Hilton Cancún guests pay discounted rates of $149 (£82) for 18 holes, or $99 (£54) for 9 holes, which includes a golf cart. Low season and twilight discounts are available. Golf clubs and shoes are available for rent. The club is open daily from 6am to 6pm and accepts American Express, MasterCard, and Visa. The **Gran Meliá Cancún** (© **998/881-1100**) has a 9-hole executive course; the fee is $53 (£29). The club is open daily from 7am to 3pm and accepts American Express, MasterCard, and Visa.

The first Jack Nicklaus Signature Golf Course in the Cancún area has opened at the **Moon Palace Spa & Golf Club** (© **998/881- 6000;** www.palaceresorts.com), along the Riviera Maya. The $260 (£143) greens fee includes cart, snacks, and drinks.

HORSEBACK RIDING

Cancún Mermaid (© **998/843-6517;** www.cancunmermaid.com), about 30 minutes south of town at the Rancho Loma Bonita, is a popular option for horseback riding. Five-hour packages include 2 hours of riding through the mangrove swamp to the beach, where you have time to swim and relax. The tour costs $72 (£40) for adults and children. The ranch also offers a four-wheel ATV ride on the same route as the horseback tour. It costs $72 (£40) per person if you want to ride on your own, $55 (£30) if you double up. Prices for both tours include transportation to the ranch, riding, soft drinks, and lunch, plus a guide and insurance. Only cash or traveler's checks are accepted.

CULTURAL ATTRACTIONS

Cancún is not a hotbed of Mexican culture, but one option is the **Museo de Arte Popular Mexicano** (© 998/849-7777), on the second floor of the El Embarcadero Marina, Bulevar Kukulkán Km 4. It displays a representative collection of masks, regional folkloric costumes, nativity scenes, religious artifacts, musical instruments, Mexican toys, and gourd art, spread over 1,370 sq. m (14,747 sq. ft.) of exhibition space. Admission is $10 (£5.50); kids younger than 12 pay half price. The museum is open daily from 11am to 11pm.

Cancún also has a small bullring, **Plaza de Toros** (© 998/884-8372; bull@prodigy.net.mx), near the northern (town) end of Bulevar Kukulkán. Bullfights take place every Wednesday at 3:30pm during the winter tourist season. A sport introduced to Mexico by the Spanish viceroys, bullfighting is now as much a part of Mexican culture as tequila. The bullfights usually include four bulls, and the spectacle begins with a folkloric dance exhibition, followed by a performance by the *charros* (Mexico's sombrero-wearing cowboys). You're not likely to see Mexico's best bullfights in Cancún—the real stars are in Mexico City. Keep in mind that if you go to a bullfight, *you're going to see a bullfight,* so stay away if you're an animal lover or you can't bear the sight of blood. Travel agencies in Cancún sell tickets, which cost $40 (£22) for adults and are free for children younger than 6; seating is by general admission. American Express, MasterCard, and Visa are accepted

3 Shopping

Despite the surrounding natural splendor, shopping has become a favorite activity. Cancún is known throughout Mexico for its diverse shops and festive malls catering to international tourists. Visitors from the United States may find apparel more expensive in Cancún, but the selection is much broader than at other Mexican resorts. Numerous duty-free shops offer excellent value on European goods. The largest is **Ultrafemme,** Avenida Tulum, Supermanzana 25 (© **998/ 884-1402**), specializing in imported cosmetics, perfumes, and fine jewelry and watches. The downtown Cancún location offers slightly lower prices than branches in Plaza Caracol and Kukulcán Plaza.

Handicrafts are more limited and more expensive in Cancún than in other regions of Mexico because they are not produced here. They are available, though; several **open-air crafts markets** are on Avenida Tulum in Cancún City and near the convention center in the Hotel Zone. One of the biggest is **Coral Negro,** Bulevar Kukulkán Km 9.5, open daily from 7am to 11pm. A small restaurant inside, Xtabentun, serves Yucatecan food and pizza, and morphs into a dance club from around 9 to 11pm.

Cancún's main venues are the **malls**—not quite as grand as their U.S. counterparts, but close. All are air-conditioned, sleek, and sophisticated. Most are on Bulevar Kukulkán between Km 7 and Km 12. They offer everything from fine crystal and silver to designer clothing and decorative objects, along with numerous restaurants and clubs. Stores are generally open daily from 10am to 10pm.

The **Kukulcán Plaza** (© **998/885-2200;** www.kukulcanplaza. com) offers a large selection—more than 300—of shops, restaurants, and entertainment. There's a bank; a theater with U.S. movies; an Internet-access kiosk; several crafts stores; a liquor and tobacco store; several bathing-suit specialty stores; record and tape outlets; a leather goods store (including shoes and sandals); and a store specializing in silver from Taxco. The Fashion Gallery features designer labels, such as Louis Vuitton, Salvatore Ferragamo, and Ultrafemme. In the food court are a number of U.S. franchises, including Ruth's Chris Steak House, plus one featuring specialty coffee. There's also a large indoor parking garage. The mall is open daily from 10am to 10pm, until 11pm during high season. Assistance for those with disabilities is available upon request, and wheelchairs, strollers, and lockers are available at the information desk.

The long-standing **Plaza Caracol** (© **998/883-1038;** www.caracol plaza.com) holds, among other things, Cartier jewelry, Señor Frog's clothing, Samsonite luggage, and La Fisheria and Casa Rolandi restaurants. It's just before you reach the convention center as you come from downtown Cancún.

Because the entertainment-oriented **Forum by the Sea,** Bulevar Kukulkán Km 9 (© **998/883-4425**), suffered extensive hurricane damage, it received a complete face-lift. Most people come here for the food and fun, choosing from Hard Rock Cafe, CoCo Bongo, and Rainforest Cafe, plus an extensive food court. Shops include Tommy Hilfiger, Diesel, Harley Davidson, Sunglass Island, and Children's World. The mall is open daily from 10am to midnight (bars remain open later).

The most intriguing mall is the **La Isla Shopping Village,** Bulevar Kukulkán Km 12.5 (© **998/883-5025;** www.laislacancun. com.mx), an open-air festival mall that looks like a small village. Walkways lined with shops and restaurants cross little canals. It also has a "riverwalk," alongside the Nichupté lagoon, and an interactive aquarium and dolphin swim facility, as well as the Spacerocker and River Ride Tour—great for kid-friendly fun. Shops include Bulgari, Diesel, DKNY, Guess, Nautica, Tommy Hilfiger, Ultrafemme, and Zara. Dining choices include Johnny Rockets, Häagen-Dazs, the fun-filled Mexican restaurant La Casa de las Margaritas, and the romantic Thai restaurant. You will also find a movie theater, video arcade, and several bars, including La Madonna.

4 Cancún After Dark

One of Cancún's main draws is its active nightlife. The hottest centers of action include **Plaza Dady'O, Forum by the Sea,** and **La Isla Shopping Village.** These places transform into spring break madness for most of March and April. Hotels also play in the nightlife scene, with happy-hour entertainment and special drink prices to entice visitors and guests from other resorts. Lobby barhopping at sunset is one way to investigate where you might want to spend next year's Cancún vacation.

THE CLUB & MUSIC SCENE

Clubbing in Cancún is a favorite part of the vacation experience and can go on each night until the sun rises over that incredibly blue sea. Several big hotels have nightclubs or schedule live music in their lobby bars. At the clubs, expect to stand in long lines on weekends, pay a cover charge of about $40 (£22) with open bar, or $15 to $25 (£8.25–£14) without open bar and then pay $8 to $10 (£4.40–£5.50) for a drink. Some of the higher-priced clubs include live entertainment. The places listed in this section are air-conditioned and accept American Express, MasterCard, and Visa.

A great idea to get you started is the **Bar Hopper Tour** 🏨🏨 with tickets available at Señor Frog's or various travel agencies around town. For $65 (£36), it takes you by bus to the Congo Bar, Dady Rock, Señor Frog's, and CoCo Bongo, where you bypass any lines and spend about an hour at each establishment. The price includes entry to the bars, one welcome drink at each, and transportation by air-conditioned bus, allowing you to get a great sampling of the best of Cancún's nightlife. The tour runs from 8pm into the wee hours, with the meeting point at the Congo Bar.

Many restaurants, such as **Carlos 'n' Charlie's, Hard Rock Cafe, Señor Frog's,** and **T.G.I. Friday's,** double as nighttime party spots, offering wildish fun at a fraction of the price of costlier clubs.

Bling 𝓡𝓡   This is one of the coolest nightspots in Cancún, featuring a chic outdoor terrace overlooking the lagoon. A fashionable 30-something crowd congregates amid sofas under the stars, a killer sound system, and flowing cocktails; a sushi and sashimi bar is also offered. This upscale lounge is considerably more sophisticated than Cancún's typical frat-style bars, and it's open daily from 9pm to 4am. Bulevar Kukulkán, Km 13.5. ✆ **998/840-6014.**

The City 𝓡𝓡𝓡   Cancún's hottest and largest nightclub, The City features progressive electronic music spun by some of the world's top DJs (the DJ station looks like an airport control tower). This is where Paris Hilton parties when she comes to town. With visiting DJs from New York, L.A., and Mexico City, the music is sizzling. You need never leave, as The City is a day-and-night club. The City Beach Club opens at 10am and features a pool with a wave machine for surfing and boogie-boarding, a tower-high waterslide, food and bar service, and beach cabañas. The Terrace Bar, overlooking the action on Bulevar Kukulkán, serves food and drinks all day. For a relaxing evening vibe, the Lounge features comfy couches, chill music, and a long menu of martinis, snacks, and desserts. Open at 10:30pm, the 2,500-sq.-m (26,910-sq.-ft.) nightclub has nine bars, stunning light shows, and several VIP areas. Bulevar Kukulkán, Km 9.5. ✆ **998/848-8380.** www.thecitycancun.com. Cover $30–$40 (£17–£22) with open bar.

CoCo Bongo 𝓡𝓡   Continuing its reputation as one of the hottest spots in town, CoCo Bongo's appeal is that it combines an enormous dance club with extravagant theme shows. It has no formal dance floor, so you can dance anywhere—and that includes on the tables, on the bar, or even on the stage with the occasional live band. This place can—and regularly does—pack in as many as 3,000 people. You have to experience it to believe it. Despite its capacity, lines are long on weekends and in high season. The music alternates between Caribbean, salsa, house, hip-hop, techno, and classics from the 1970s, '80s, and '90s. Open from 10:30pm to 3:30am, CoCo

Bongo draws a hip young crowd. Forum by the Sea, Bulevar Kukulkán Km 9.5. ℂ **998/883-5061**. www.cocobongo.com.mx. Cover $40–$45 (£22–£25) with open bar.

Dady'O   This is a popular rave among the young and brave with frequent long lines. It opens nightly at 10pm and has a giant dance floor and awesome light system. Bulevar Kukulkán Km 9.5. ℂ **998/883-3333**. www.dadyo.net. Cover $20 (£11); $40 (£22) with open bar.

Dady Rock Bar and Grill   The offspring of Dady'O, it opens at 7pm and goes as long as any other nightspot, offering a combination of live bands and DJs spinning music, along with an open bar, full meals, a buffet, and dancing. Bulevar Kukulkán Km 9.5. ℂ **998/883-1626**. Cover $16 (£8.80); $35 (£19) with open bar

La Madonna   This martini bar and restaurant emerges unexpectedly from La Isla shopping center like a chic gem along the canal. With over 180 creative martini selections accompanied by relaxing lounge music, La Madonna also offers authentic Italian and Swiss cuisine. Enjoy your red mandarin, lychee, or vanilla peach martini elbow to elbow with Cancún's beautiful people on one of the red leather chairs on the expansive patio. It's open daily from noon to 1am. La Isla Shopping Village, Bulevar Kukulkán Km 12.5. ℂ **998/883-2222**.

The Lobby Lounge ⭐   This is the most refined and upscale of Cancún's nightly gathering spots, with a terrace overlooking the lagoon, a special martini collection, and a list of more than 80 premium tequilas for tasting or sipping. There's also a sushi and seafood bar, as well as a humidor collection of Cuban cigars. It's open daily from 5pm to 1am, with live music Thursday through Sunday. Ritz-Carlton Cancún, Retorno del Rey 36, off Bulevar Kukulkán Km 13.5. ℂ **998/881-0808**.

THE PERFORMING ARTS

Several hotels host **Mexican fiesta nights,** including a buffet dinner and a folkloric dance show; admission, including dinner, ranges from $35 to $50 (£19–£28), unless you're at an all-inclusive resort that includes this as part of the package.

Tourists mingle with locals at the downtown **Parque de las Palapas** (the main park) for Noches Caribeñas, which involves children-oriented performances (such as clown shows) and free live tropical music. Performances begin at 7:30pm on Sunday, and sometimes there are events on Friday and Saturday.

4

Day Trips: Island Getaways & Nature Parks

One of the best ways to spend a vacation day is exploring the nearby archaeological ruins or an ecological theme park near Cancún. Within easy driving distance are historical and natural treasures unlike any you've likely encountered before. Cancún can be a perfect base for day or overnight trips, or the starting point for a longer expedition. This chapter discusses **Isla Mujeres, Xel-Ha,** and **Xcaret.** For those who want to get a way from it all, I've also included information about the rustic natural beauty of the **Punta Allen Peninsula.** For information on the Maya ruins to the south at **Tulum** or **Cobá,** see chapter 5.

1 Isla Mujeres ★★★

13km (8 miles) N of Cancún

Isla Mujeres (Island of Women) is a casual, laid-back refuge from the conspicuously commercialized action of Cancún, visible across a narrow channel. It's known as the best value in the Caribbean, assuming that you favor an easygoing vacation pace and prefer simplicity to pretense. This is an island of white-sand beaches and turquoise waters, complemented by a town filled with Caribbean-colored clapboard houses and rustic, open-air restaurants. Most hotels here are clean, comfortable and beachy, with a few luxury boutique hotels dotting the island. But, in general, if you're looking for lots of action or opulence, you're likely to prefer Cancún.

Francisco Hernández de Córdoba, seeing figurines of partially clad females along the shore, gave the island its name when he landed in 1517. These are now believed to have been offerings to the Maya goddess of fertility and the moon, Ixchel. Their presence indicates that the island was probably sacred to the Maya.

At midday, suntanned visitors hang out in open-air cafes and stroll pedestrian streets lined with zealous souvenir vendors. Calling

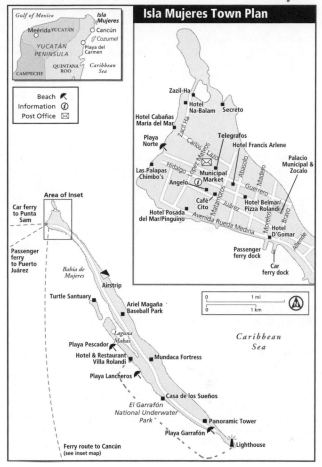

Isla Mujeres Town Plan

Gulf of Mexico

Isla
Mujeres

Meérida YUCATÁN

YUCATÁN
PENINSULA

CAMPECHE

QUINTANA
ROO

Cancún

Cozumel

Playa del
Carmen

Caribbean
Sea

Beach
Information ⓘ
Post Office ✉

Area of Inset

Car ferry
to Punta
Sam

Passenger
ferry
to Puerto
Juárez

Bahía de
Mujeres

Zazil-Ha

Hotel
Na-Balam

Secreto

Hotel Cabañas
María del Mar

Zazil Ha

Carlos Lazo

López Mateos

Playa
Norte

Telegrafos

Hotel Francis Arlene

Palacio
Municipal &
Zocalo

Hidalgo

Las Palapas
Chimbo's

Angelo

Municipal
Market ⓘ

Abasolo

Madero

Guerrero

Bravo

Morelos

Allende

Café
Cito

Matamoros

Juárez

Hotel Belmar/
Pizza Rolandi

Hotel Posada
del Mar/Pinguino

Avenida Rueda Medina

Hotel
D'Gomar

Passenger
ferry dock

Car
ferry dock

Airstrip

Turtle Sanctuary

Ariel Magaña
Baseball Park

Laguna
Makax

Caribbean
Sea

Playa Pescador

Hotel & Restaurant
Villa Rolandi

Mundaca Fortress

Playa Lancheros 🏖

Casa de los Sueños

El Garrafón
National Underwater
Park

Panoramic Tower

Playa Garrafón

Ferry route to Cancún
(see inset map)

Lighthouse

0   1 mi
0   1 km

attention to their bargain-priced wares, they give a carnival atmosphere to the hours when tour-boat traffic is at its peak. Befitting the size of the island, most of the traffic consists of golf carts, *motos* (mopeds), and bicycles. Once the tour boats leave, however, Isla Mujeres reverts to its more typical, tranquil way of life.

Days in "Isla"—as the locals call it—can alternate between adventurous activity and absolute repose. Trips to the Isla Contoy bird sanctuary are popular, as are the excellent diving, fishing, and snorkeling—in 1998, the island's coral coast became part of Mexico's Marine National Park system. Although the reef suffered substantial hurricane damage in 2005, it is now largely back to normal. The incredible water clarity illuminates the wonderful array of coral and tropical fish living here. Among the underwater life you are likely to see are French angelfish, longspine squirrelfish, trumpet fish, four-eye butterfly fish, green angelfish, stoplight parrotfish, southern stingrays, sharp-nose puffer fish, blue tang, and great barracuda.

An upside of Hurricane Wilma's impact is that Playa Norte received an infusion of white sand, and is now broader and more beautiful than ever, despite the "haircuts" suffered by many of the palm trees. The island and several of its traditional hotels attract regular gatherings of yoga practitioners. In the evening, most people find the slow, casual pace one of the island's biggest draws. The cool night breeze is a perfect accompaniment to casual open-air dining and drinking in small street-side restaurants. Many people pack it in as early as 9 or 10pm, when most of the businesses close. Those in search of a party, however, will find kindred souls at the bars on Playa Norte that stay open late.

ESSENTIALS

GETTING THERE & DEPARTING   Puerto Juárez, just north of Cancún, is the **dock** (© **998/877-0382**) for passenger ferries to Isla Mujeres. *Ultramar* (© **998/843-2011;** www.granpuerto. com.mx) has fast boats leaving every half-hour from "Gran Puerto" in Puerto Juárez, making the trip in 15 minutes. There is storage space for luggage and the fare is about $4 (£2.20) each way. These boats operate daily, starting at 6am and usually ending at 10:30pm (check beforehand for latest schedules). They might leave early if they're full, so arrive ahead of schedule. Pay at the ticket office—or, if the ferry is about to leave, aboard.

Note: Upon arrival by taxi or bus in Puerto Juárez, be wary of pirate "guides" who tell you either that the ferry is canceled or that it's several hours until the next ferry. They'll offer the services of a private *lancha* (small boat) for about $40 (£22)—and it's nothing but a scam. Small boats are available and, on a co-op basis, charge $15 to $25 (£8.25–£14) one-way, based on the number of passengers. They take about 50 minutes and are not recommended on days with rough seas. Check with the clearly visible ticket office—the only accurate source for information.

Taxi fares are posted by the street where the taxis park, so be sure to check the rate before agreeing to a taxi for the ride back to Cancún. Rates generally run $12 to $15 (£6.60–£8.25), depending upon your destination. Moped and bicycle rentals are also readily available as you depart the ferry. This small complex also has public bathrooms, luggage storage, a snack bar, and souvenir shops.

Isla Mujeres is so small that a vehicle isn't necessary, but if you're taking one, you'll use the **Punta Sam** port a little beyond Puerto Juárez. The 40-minute car ferry (© **998/877-0065**) runs five or six times daily between 8am and 8pm, year-round except in bad weather. Times are generally as follows: Cancún to Isla 8 and 11am and 2:45, 5:30, and 8:15pm; Isla to Cancún 6:30 and 9:30am and 12:45, 4:15, and 7:15pm. Always check with the tourist office in Cancún to verify this schedule. Cars should arrive an hour before the ferry departure to register for a place in line and pay the posted fee, which varies depending on the weight and type of vehicle. A gas pump in Isla is at the intersection of Avenida Rueda Medina and Calle Abasolo, just northwest of the ferry docks.

There are also ferries to Isla Mujeres from the **Playa Linda,** known as the Embarcadero pier in Cancún, but they're less frequent and more expensive than those from Puerto Juárez. A **Water Taxi** (© **998/ 886-4270** or -4847; asterix@cablered.net.mx) to Isla Mujeres runs from **Playa Caracol,** between the Fiesta Americana Coral Beach Hotel and the Xcaret terminal on the island, with prices about the same as those from Playa Linda and about four times the cost of the public ferries from Puerto Juárez. Scheduled departures are at 9 and 11am and 1pm, with returns from Isla Mujeres at noon and 5pm. Adult round-trip fares are $15 (£8.25); kids ages 3 to 12 pay $7.50 (£4.15), free for children younger than 3.

To get to Puerto Juárez or Punta Sam from **Cancún,** take any Ruta 8 city bus from Avenida Tulum. If you're coming from **Mérida,** you can fly to Cancún and proceed to Puerto Juárez, or take a bus directly to Puerto Juárez. From **Cozumel,** you can fly to Cancún (there are daily flights), or take a ferry to Playa del Carmen and then travel to Puerto Juárez.

Arriving   Passenger ferries arrive at the docks in the center of town (car ferries arrive just north of town). The main road that passes in front is Avenida Rueda Medina. Most hotels are close by. Tricycle taxis are the least expensive and most fun way to get to your hotel; you and your luggage pile in the open carriage compartment, and the driver pedals through the streets. Regular taxis are always lined up in a parking lot to the right of the pier, with their rates posted. If someone on the ferry offers to arrange a taxi for you, politely decline, unless you'd like some help with your luggage down the short pier—it just means an extra, unnecessary tip for your helper.

VISITOR INFORMATION   The **City Tourist Office** (℃/fax **998/ 877-0767** or -0307) is at Av. Rueda Medina 130, just across the street from the pier. It's open Monday through Friday from 9am to 4pm, closed on Saturdays and Sundays. Also look for *Islander,* a free publication with local information, advertisements, and event listings.

ISLAND LAYOUT   Isla Mujeres is about 8km (5 miles) long and 4km (2½ miles) wide, with the town at the northern tip. "Downtown" is a compact 4 blocks by 6 blocks, so it's very easy to get around. The **passenger ferry docks** are at the center of town, within walking distance of most hotels, restaurants, and shops. The street running along the waterfront is **Avenida Rueda Medina,** commonly called the *malecón* **(boardwalk).** The **Mercado Municipal (town market)** is by the post office on **Calle Guerrero,** an inland street at the north edge of town, which, like most streets in the town, is unmarked.

GETTING AROUND   A popular form of transportation on Isla Mujeres is the electric **golf cart,** available for rent at many hotels or rental shops for $15 (£8.25) per hour or $45 (£25) per day. Prices are set the same at all rental locations. **El Sol Golf Cart Rental,** Av. Benito Juárez Mza 3 #20 (corner of Matamoros; ℃ **998/877-0791**) is one good option in the town center. The golf carts don't go more than 30kmph (20 mph), but they're fun. Anyway, you aren't on Isla Mujeres to hurry. Many people enjoy touring the island by *moto* **(motorized bike or scooter).** Fully automatic versions are available for around $30 (£17) per day or $8 (£4.40) per hour. They come with helmets and seats for two people. There's only one main road with a couple of offshoots, so you won't get lost. Be aware that the rental price does not include insurance, and any injury to yourself or the vehicle will come out of your pocket. **Bicycles** are also available for rent at some hotels for $4 (£2.20) per hour or $10 (£5.50) per day, usually including a basket and a lock.

   If you prefer to use a taxi, rates are about $2.50 (£1.40) for trips within the downtown area, or $4.50 (£2.50) for a trip to the southern end of Isla. You can also hire them for about $10 (£5.50) per hour. The number to call for taxis is ℃ **998/877-0066.**

FAST FACTS: Isla Mujeres

Area Code The telephone area code is **998**.

Consumer Protection You can reach the local branch of **Profeco** consumer protection agency at © **998/887-3960**.

Currency Exchange Isla Mujeres has numerous *casas de cambio*, or currency exchanges, that you can easily spot along the main streets. Most of the hotels listed here change money for their guests, although often at less favorable rates than the commercial enterprises. There is only one bank in Isla, **HSBC Bank** (© 998/877-0005), across from the ferry docks. It's open Monday through Friday from 8:30am to 6pm, and Saturdays from 9am to 2pm.

Drugstore **Isla Mujeres Farmacía** (© 998/877-0178) has the best selection of prescription and over-the-counter medicines.

Emergencies To report an emergency, dial © **065** from any phone within Mexico.

Hospital The **Hospital de la Armada** is on Avenida Rueda Medina at Ojón P. Blanco (© 998/877-0001). It's less than a kilometer (a half-mile) south of the town center. It will only treat you in an emergency. Otherwise, you're referred to the **Centro de Salud** on Avenida Guerrero, a block before the beginning of the *malecón* (© 998/877-0117).

Internet Access Owned by a lifelong resident of Isla, **Cyber Isla Mujeres.com,** Av. Francisco y Madero 17, between Hidalgo and Juárez streets (© 998/877-0272), offers Internet access for $1.50 (85p) per hour, daily 7am to 10pm, and serves complimentary Veracruzano coffee all day.

Post Office The *correo* is at Calle Guerrero 12 (© 998/877-0085), at the corner of López Mateos, near the market. It's open Monday through Friday from 9am to 4pm.

Taxis To call for a taxi, dial © **998/877-0066**.

Telephone Ladatel phones accepting coins and prepaid phone cards are at the plaza and throughout town. Also see area code, above.

Tourist Seasons Isla Mujeres's tourist season (when hotel rates are higher) is a bit different from that of other places in Mexico. High season runs December through May, a month longer than in Cancún. Some hotels raise their rates in August, and some raise their rates beginning in mid-November. Low season is from June to mid-November.

BEACHES & OUTDOOR ACTIVITIES

THE BEACHES   The most popular beach in town is **Playa Norte** ☆. The long stretch of beach extends around the northern tip of the island, to your left as you get off the boat. This is perhaps the world's best municipal beach—a wide swath of fine white sand and calm, translucent, turquoise-blue water. The beach is easily reached on foot from the ferry and from all downtown hotels. Watersports equipment, beach umbrellas, and lounge chairs are available for rent. Areas in front of restaurants usually cost nothing if you use the restaurant as your headquarters for drinks and food, and the best of them have hammocks and swings from which to sip your piña coladas.

Garrafón Natural Reef Park ☆☆ (see "Snorkeling," below) is best known as a snorkeling area, but there is a nice stretch of beach on either side of the park. **Playa Lancheros** is on the Caribbean side of Laguna Makax. Local buses go to Lancheros, and then turn inland and return downtown. The beach at Playa Lancheros is nice, with a variety of casual restaurants.

SWIMMING   Wide Playa Norte is the best swimming beach, with Playa Lancheros second. There are no lifeguards on duty on Isla Mujeres, which does not use the system of water-safety flags employed in Cancún and Cozumel. The bay between Cancún and Isla Mujeres is calm, with warm, transparent waters ideal for swimming, snorkeling, and diving. The east side of the island facing the open Caribbean Sea is rougher with much stronger currents.

SNORKELING   The most popular place to snorkel is **Garrafón Natural Reef Park** ☆☆ (ⓒ **998/849-4748;** www.garrafon.com). It lies at the southern end of the island, where you'll see numerous schools of colorful fish. The pricey but well-equipped park has two restaurant/bars, beach chairs, a swimming pool, kayaks, changing rooms, rental lockers, showers, a gift shop, and snack bars. Once a public national underwater park, Garrafón is now operated by a private company. Public facilities have been vastly improved, with new attractions and facilities added each year. Activities at the park include snorkeling and Snuba (a tankless version of scuba diving, in which you descend while breathing through a long air tube), "Sea Trek," which allows you to explore the Caribbean seabed wearing a helmet with compressed air, crystal-clear canoes for viewing underwater life, and a zip-line that takes you over the water. On land, there are tanning decks, shaded hammocks, a 12m (40-ft.) climbing tower, and—of course!—a souvenir superstore. Several restaurants and snack bars are available. Admission for the Garrafón Discovery package (required for entry) includes sea transfer from Cancún, continental breakfast, open bar, lunch buffet, and snorkeling equipment for $65 (£36) for adults, $49 (£27) for children (American Express, MasterCard, and Visa are accepted). More expensive packages include swims with dolphins at Dolphin Discovery. The park is open daily from 9am to 5pm.

Also good for snorkeling is **Manchones Reef,** off the southeastern coast. The reef is just offshore and accessible by boat.

Another excellent location is around *el faro* (the lighthouse) in the **Bahía de Mujeres** at the southern tip of the island, where the water is about 2m (6½ ft.) deep. Boatmen will take you for around $25 (£14) per person if you have your own snorkeling equipment or $30 (£17) if you use theirs.

DIVING   Most of the dive shops on the island offer the same trips for the same prices: One-tank dives cost about $50 (£28), two-tank dives about $70 (£38.50). **Bahía Dive Shop,** Rueda Medina 166, across from the car-ferry dock (*©* **998/877-0340**), is a full-service shop that offers dive equipment for sale or rent. The shop is open daily from 10am to 7pm, and accepts MasterCard and Visa. Another respected dive shop is **Coral Scuba Center,** at Matamoros 13A and Rueda Medina (*©* **998/877-0061** or -0763). It's open daily from 8am to 12:30pm and 4 to 10pm. Both offer 2-hour snorkeling trips for about $20 (£11).

Cuevas de los Tiburones (Caves of the Sleeping Sharks) is Isla's most renowned dive site—but the name is slightly misleading, as shark sightings are rare these days. Two sites where you could traditionally see the sleeping shark are the Cuevas de Tiburones and **La Punta,** but the sharks have mostly been driven off, and a storm collapsed the arch featured in a Jacques Cousteau film showing them, but the caves survive. Other dive sites include a **wreck** 15km (9⅓ miles) offshore; **Banderas** reef, between Isla Mujeres and Cancún, where there's always a strong current; **Tabos** reef on the eastern shore; and **Manchones** reef, 1km (a half-mile) off the southeastern tip of the island, where the water is 4.5 to 11m (15–36 ft.) deep. **The Cross of the Bay** is close to Manchones reef. A bronze cross, weighing 1 ton and standing 12m (40 ft.) high, was placed in the water between Manchones and Isla in 1994, as a memorial to those who have lost their lives at sea.

FISHING   To arrange a day of fishing, ask at the **Sociedad Cooperativa Turística** (the boatmen's cooperative), on Avenida Rueda Medina (© **998/877-1363**), next to Mexico Divers and Las Brisas restaurant, or the travel agency mentioned in "A Visit to Isla Contoy," below. Four to six others can share the cost, which includes lunch and drinks. Captain Tony Martínez (© **998/877-0274**) also arranges fishing trips aboard the *Marinonis,* with advanced reservations recommended. Year-round you'll find bonito, mackerel, kingfish, and amberjack. Sailfish and sharks (hammerhead, bull, nurse, lemon, and tiger) are in good supply in April and May. In winter, larger grouper and jewfish are prevalent. Four hours of fishing close to shore costs around $110 (£61); 8 hours farther out goes for $250 (£138). The cooperative is open Monday through Saturday from 8am to 1pm and 5 to 8pm, and Sunday from 7:30 to 10am and 6 to 8pm.

YOGA   Increasingly, Isla is becoming known as a great place to combine a relaxing beach vacation with yoga practice and instruction. The trend began at **Hotel Na Balam** 🐟🐟 (© **998/877-0279** or -0058; www.nabalam.com), which offers yoga classes under its large poolside *palapa,* complete with yoga mats and props. The classes, which begin at 9am Monday through Friday, are free to guests, $15 (£8.25) per class to visitors. Na Balam is also the site of frequent yoga instruction vacations featuring respected teachers and a more extensive practice schedule; the current schedule of yoga retreats is posted on their website. Local yoga culture extends down the island to **Casa de los Sueños Resort and Zenter** (© **998/877-0651;** www.casadelossuenosresort.com), where yoga classes, as well as chi gong and Pilates, are regularly held.

MORE ATTRACTIONS
DOLPHIN DISCOVERY 🐟🐟   You can swim with live dolphins (© **998/877-0207** or 849-4757; fax 998/849-4751; www.dolphin discovery.com) in an enclosure at Treasure Island, on the side of Isla Mujeres that faces Cancún. Groups .of eight people swim with two dolphins and one trainer. Swimmers view an educational video and spend time in the water with the trainer and the dolphins before 15 minutes of free swimming time. Reservations are recommended, and you must arrive an hour before your assigned swimming time, at 10:30am, noon, 2 or 3:30pm. The cost is $139 (£76) per person for the Dolphin Royal Swim. There are less-expensive programs that allow you to learn about, touch, and hold the dolphins (but not swim with them) starting at $79 (£43).

Swimming with Flipper

The popularity of dolphin swims grows yearly, as does the swell of controversy surrounding the activity. Animal rights activists contend that captivity shortens the life span of these keenly intelligent creatures, as does the stress of interacting with humans. The **Whale & Dolphin Conservation Society** (www.wdcs.org) offers information to help you know what questions to ask before you decide whether to take the plunge.

A TURTLE SANCTUARY 🐢🐢   As recently as 20 years ago, fishermen converged on the island nightly from May to September, waiting for the monster-size turtles to lumber ashore to deposit their Ping-Pong-ball–shaped eggs. Totally vulnerable once they begin laying their eggs, and exhausted when they have finished, the turtles were easily captured and slaughtered for their highly prized meat, shell, and eggs. Then a concerned fisherman, Gonzalez Cahle Maldonado, began convincing others to spare at least the eggs, which he protected. It was a start. Following his lead, the fishing secretariat founded the **Centro de Investigaciones;** although the local government provided assistance in the past, now the center relies solely on private donations. Since opening, tens of thousands of turtles have been released, and every year local schoolchildren participate in the event, thus planting the notion of protecting the turtles for a new generation of islanders.

Six species of sea turtles nest on Isla Mujeres. An adult green turtle, the most abundant species, measures 1 to 1.5m (3¼–5 ft.) in length and can weigh 450 pounds. At the center, visitors walk through the indoor and outdoor turtle pool areas, where the creatures paddle around. The turtles are separated by age, from newly hatched up to 1 year. People who come here usually end up staying at least an hour, especially if they opt for the guided tour, which I recommend. They also have a small gift shop and snack bar. The sanctuary is on a piece of land separated from the island by Bahía de Mujeres and Laguna Makax, at Carr. Sac Bajo #5; you'll need a taxi to get there. Admission is $3 (£1.65); the shelter is open daily from 9am to 5pm. For more information, call ✆ **998/877-0595.**

SIGHTS OF PUNTA SUR 🐢🐢   At Punta Sur (the southern point of the island, just inland from **Garrafón National Reef Park;** call ✆ **998/877-1100** or go to www.garrafon.com), and part of the park, is Isla's newest attraction, the **Panoramic Tower.** At 50m (164 ft.)

high, the tower offers visitors a bird's-eye view of the entire island. The tower holds 20 visitors at a time, and rotates for 10 minutes while you snap photos or simply enjoy the scenery. However, it was closed for renovations at press time.

Next to the tower you'll find **Sculptured Spaces,** an impressive and extensive garden of large sculptures donated to Isla Mujeres by internationally renowned sculptors as part of the 2001 First International Sculpture Exhibition. Among Mexican sculptors represented by works are José Luis Cuevas and Vladimir Cora.

Nearby is the **Caribbean Village,** with narrow lanes of colorful clapboard buildings that house cafes and shops displaying folkloric art. Plan to have lunch or a snack here at the kiosk and stroll around, before heading on to the lighthouse and Maya ruins.

Also at this southern point of the island, and part of the ruins, is **Cliff of the Dawn,** the southeasternmost point of Mexico. Services are available from 9am to 5pm, but you can enter at any time; if you make it there early enough to see the sunrise, you can claim you were the first person in Mexico that day to be touched by the sun!

A MAYA RUIN 🐦🐦   Just beyond the lighthouse, at the southern end of the island, are the strikingly beautiful remains of a small Maya temple, believed to have been built to pay homage to the moon and fertility goddess Ixchel. The location, on a lofty bluff overlooking the sea, is worth seeing and makes a great place for photos. It is believed that Maya women traveled here on annual pilgrimages to seek Ixchel's blessings of fertility. From Garrafón park, it's not too far a walk. Turn right from Garrafón. When you see the lighthouse, turn toward it down the rocky path.

A PIRATE'S FORTRESS   The Fortress of Mundaca is about 4km (2½ miles) in the same direction as Garrafón, less than a kilometer (about half a mile) to the left. A slave trader who claimed to have been the pirate Mundaca Marecheaga built the fortress. In the early 19th century, he arrived at Isla Mujeres and set up a blissful paradise, while making money selling slaves to Cuba and Belize. According to island lore, he settled down and built this hacienda after being captivated by the charms of an island girl. However, she reputedly spurned his affections and married another islander, leaving him heartbroken and alone on Isla Mujeres. Admission is $2 (£1.10); the fortress is open daily from 10am to 6pm.

A VISIT TO ISLA CONTOY 🐦   If possible, plan to visit this pristine uninhabited island—30km (20 miles) by boat from Isla

Mujeres—that became a national wildlife reserve in 1981. Lush vegetation covers the oddly shaped island, which is 6km (3¾ miles) long and harbors 70 species of birds as well as a host of marine and animal life. Bird species that nest on the island include pelicans, brown boobies, frigates, egrets, terns, and cormorants. Flocks of flamingos arrive in April. June, July, and August are good months to spot turtles burying their eggs in the sand at night. Most excursions troll for fish (which will be your lunch), anchor en route for a snorkeling expedition, skirt the island at a leisurely pace for close viewing of the birds without disturbing the habitat, and then pull ashore. While the captain prepares lunch, visitors can swim, sun, follow the nature trails, and visit the fine nature museum, which has bathroom facilities. The trip from Isla Mujeres takes about 45 minutes each way and can be longer if the waves are choppy. Because of the tight-knit boatmen's cooperative, prices for this excursion are the same everywhere: $40 (£22). You can buy a ticket at the **Sociedad Cooperativa Turística** on Avenida Rueda Medina, next to Mexico Divers and Las Brisas restaurant (© **998/877-1363**). Isla Contoy trips leave at 9am and return around 4:30pm. The price (cash only) is $55 (£30) for adults, $28 (£15) for children. Boat captains should respect the cooperative's regulations regarding ecological sensitivity and boat safety, including the availability of life jackets for everyone on board. If you're not given a life jacket, ask for one. Snorkeling equipment is usually included in the price, but double-check before heading out.

SHOPPING

Shopping is a casual activity here. There are only a few shops of any sophistication. Shop owners will bombard you, especially on Avenida Hidalgo, selling Saltillo rugs, onyx, silver, Guatemalan clothing, blown glassware, masks, folk art, beach paraphernalia, and T-shirts in abundance. Prices are lower than in Cancún or Cozumel, but with such overeager sellers, bargaining is necessary.

The one treasure you're likely to take back is a piece of fine jewelry—Isla is known for its excellent, duty-free prices on gemstones and handcrafted work made to order. Diamonds, emeralds, sapphires, and rubies can be purchased as loose stones and then mounted while you're off exploring. The superbly crafted gold, silver, and gems are available at very competitive prices in the workshops near the central plaza. The stones are also available in the rough. **Von Hauste** (© **998/877-0331**) located at the corner of

Morelos and Juárez streets, is the grandest store, with a broad selection of jewelry including diamonds, emeralds, sapphires, and tanzanites at competitive prices. It's open daily from 9am to 5:30pm and accepts all major credit cards.

WHERE TO STAY

You'll find plenty of hotels in all price ranges on Isla Mujeres. Rates peak during high season, which is the most expensive and most crowded time to go. Elizabeth Wenger of **Yucatan Peninsula Travel** in Montello, Wisconsin (© **800/552-4550** in the U.S.), specializes in Mexico travel and books a lot of hotels in Isla Mujeres. Her service is invaluable in the high season. Those interested in private home rentals or longer-term stays can contact **Mundaca Travel and Real Estate** in Isla Mujeres (© **998/877-0025;** fax 998/877-0076; www.mundaca.com.mx), or book online with **Isla Beckons** property rental service (www.islabeckons.com).

VERY EXPENSIVE

Casa de los Sueños Resort & Spa Zenter ✸✸✸   This "house of dreams" is easily Isla Mujeres's most intimate, sophisticated, and relaxing property. Though it was originally built as a private residence, luckily it became an upscale, adults-only boutique hotel in early 1998 (it has since changed ownership), and now caters to guests looking for a rejuvenating experience, with the adjoining Zenter offering spa services and yoga classes. Its location on the southern end of the island, adjacent to Garrafón Natural Reef Park, also makes it ideal for snorkeling and diving enthusiasts. The captivating design features vivid sherbet-colored walls—think watermelon, mango, and blueberry—and a sculpted architecture. There's a large, open interior courtyard; tropical gardens; a sunken living area (with Wi-Fi access); and an infinity pool that melts into the cool Caribbean waters. All rooms have balconies or terraces and face west, offering stunning views of the sunset over the sea, as well as the night lights of Cancún. In addition, the rooms—which have names such as Serenity, Peace, and Love—also have large marble bathrooms, Egyptian cotton bedding, and luxury bath amenities, and they are decorated in a serene style that blends Asian simplicity with Mexican details. One master suite ideal for honeymooners has an exceptionally spacious bathroom area, complete with whirlpool and steam room/shower, plus other deluxe amenities. Complimentary continental breakfast is served in your room, and a restaurant adjacent to their private pier serves healthful fusion cuisine—it's open to nonguests as well. The Zenter offers a very complete menu of massages and holistic spa treatments, as well as yoga classes, held either outdoors or in a serene indoor space.

Carretera Garrafón s/n, 77400 Isla Mujeres, Q. Roo. ⓒ **998/877-0651** or -0369. Fax 998/877-0708. www.casadelossuenosresort.com. 9 units. High season $350–$450 (£193–£248) double; low season $300–$400 (£165–£220) double. Rates include continental breakfast and taxes. MC, V. No children younger than 15. **Amenities:** Restaurant; infinity pool; spa; open-air massage area; room service; yoga center. *In room:* TV/VCR, hair dryer, iron, safe.

Hotel Villa Rolandi Gourmet & Beach Club ★★★ *Moments*

Set on the Caribbean like a hidden jewel, Villa Rolandi is a romantic escape on one of Mexico's most idyllic islands. A private yacht brings the privileged guests from Cancún directly to the hotel, which lies on a sheltered cove with a pristine white-sand beach, interrupted only by a sailboat and set of kayaks waiting to be taken to the sea. Each of the luxurious suites holds a separate sitting area and large terrace or balcony with private whirlpool overlooking the sea. Flatscreen TVs offer satellite music and movies, and all rooms feature sophisticated in-room sound systems, subtle lighting, and deep-hued Tikal marble. The beautiful bathrooms have Bulgari products and enticing showers with multiple showerheads that convert into steam baths. In-room breakfast is delivered through a small closet-like door. The luxurious hotel spa also offers an outdoor Thalasso therapy whirlpool and beachside massages.

Dining is an integral part of a stay at Villa Rolandi. The owner is a Swiss-born restaurateur who made a name for himself with his restaurants on Isla Mujeres and in Cancún (see **Casa Rolandi** and **Pizza Rolandi** under "Where to Dine," below). This intimate hideaway is ideal for honeymooners, who receive a complimentary bottle of domestic champagne upon arrival (when the hotel is notified in advance). Service throughout this beautiful property is gracious and refined.

Fracc. Lagunamar, SM 7, Mza. 75, Locs. 15 and 16, 77400 Isla Mujeres, Q. Roo. ⓒ **998/ 877-0700.** Fax 998/877-0100. www.villarolandi.com. 28 units. High season $380–$450 (£209–£248) double; low season $290–$350 (£160–£193) double. Rates include round-trip transportation from Playa Linda in Cancún aboard private catamaran yacht, continental breakfast, and a la carte lunch or dinner in the on-site restaurant. AE, MC, V. Children younger than 13 not accepted. **Amenities:** Restaurant (see "Where to Dine," below); infinity pool w/waterfall; small fitness room and open-air massage area; concierge; tour desk; room service. *In room:* TV, Wi-Fi, minibar, hair dryer, iron, safe.

EXPENSIVE

Hotel Na Balam 🌟🌟 *(Finds)* Na Balam is known as a haven for yoga students and those interested in an introspective vacation. This popular, two-story hotel near the end of Playa Norte has comfortable rooms on a quiet, ideally located portion of the beach. Rooms are in three sections; some face the beach, and others are across the street in a garden setting with a swimming pool. All rooms have a terrace or balcony with hammocks. Each spacious suite contains a king-size or two double beds, a seating area, and folk-art decorations. Master suites have additional amenities, including small pools with hydromassage situated under coconut trees—ask if these are available for the best of Na Balam. Though other rooms are newer, the older section is well kept, with a bottom-floor patio facing the peaceful, palm-filled, sandy inner yard and Playa Norte. Yoga classes (free for guests; $15/£8.25 per class for nonguests) start at 9am Monday through Friday. The restaurant, **Zazil Ha,** is one of the island's most popular (see "Where to Dine," below). A beachside bar serves a selection of natural juices and is one of the most popular spots for sunset watching.

Zazil Ha 118, 77400 Isla Mujeres, Q. Roo. © **998/877-0279.** Fax 998/877-0446. www.nabalam.com. 33 units. High season $240–$450 (£132–£248) suite; low season $180–$388 (£99–£213) suite. Ask about weekly and monthly rates. AE, MC, V. **Amenities:** 2 restaurants; 2 bars; outdoor swimming pool; yoga classes; spa; mopeds, golf carts, and bikes for rent; game room w/TV; salon; in-room massage; babysitting; laundry service; diving and snorkeling trips available; Wi-Fi. *In room:* A/C, fan.

Secreto 🌟🌟 *(Finds)* This boutique hotel resembles a chic Mediterranean villa and is one of the best B&B values in the Caribbean. It offers nine suites that overlook an infinity-edge pool and the open sea beyond. Located on the northern end of the island, Secreto lies within walking distance of town, yet feels removed enough to make for an idyllic retreat. Tropical gardens surround the pool area, and an outdoor living area offers comfy couches and places to dine. Guest rooms are characterized by contemporary designs featuring clean, white spaces and original artwork. Each features a veranda with private cabaña ideal for ocean-gazing beyond Halfmoon Beach. Three suites include king-size beds draped in mosquito netting, while the remaining six have two double beds; all rooms are nonsmoking. Transportation from Cancún airport can be arranged on request, for an additional $50 (£28) per van (not per person). Secreto is distinguished by its stunning and secluded location and gracious service.

Sección Rocas, Lote 1, 77400 Isla Mujeres, Q. Roo. © **998/877-1039.** Fax 998/ 877-1048. www.hotelsecreto.com. 9 units. $225–$250 (£124–£138) double. Extra person $25 (£14). 1 child younger than 5 stays free in parent's room. Rates include continental breakfast. AE, MC, V. **Amenities:** Outdoor pool; private cove beach; tours, diving, and snorkeling available; dinner delivery from Rolandi's restaurant available. *In room:* A/C, TV, fridge, safe, CD player, bathrobes.

MODERATE

Hotel Cabañas María del Mar ⓡ   A good choice for simple beach accommodations, the Cabañas María del Mar is on the popular Playa Norte. The older two-story section behind the reception area and beyond the garden offers nicely outfitted rooms facing the beach. All have two single or double beds, refrigerators, and ocean-view balconies strung with hammocks. Eleven single-story cabañas closer to the reception area are decorated in a rustic Mexican style. The third section, **El Castillo,** is located across the street, over and beside Buho's restaurant. It contains all "deluxe" rooms, but some are larger than others; the five rooms on the ground floor have large patios. Upstairs rooms have small balconies. Most have ocean views and predominately white decor. The lush central courtyard contains a small pool and enchanting lighting at night.

Av. Arq. Carlos Lazo 1 (on Playa Norte, one-half block from the Hotel Na Balam), 77400 Isla Mujeres, Q. Roo. ⓒ 800/223-5695 in the U.S., or 998/877-0179. Fax 998/877-0213. www.cabanasdelmar.com. 73 units. High season $121–$133 (£67–£73) double; low season $75–$99 (£41–£54) double. MC, V. **Amenities:** Outdoor pool; bus for tours and boat for rent; golf cart and *moto* rentals. *In room:* A/C, fridge.

INEXPENSIVE

Hotel Belmar ⓡⓡ   Situated in the center of Isla's small-town activity, this charming hotel sits above Pizza Rolandi (be sure to consider the restaurant noise) and is run by the same people. Each of the simple but stylish tile-accented rooms comes with two twin or double beds. Prices are a bit high considering the lack of views, but the rooms are appealing. This is one of the few island hotels that offer televisions (with U.S. channels) in rooms. It has one large colonial-decorated suite with a sitting area, large patio, and whirlpool. Note that most rooms are accessed by a series of stairs.

Av. Hidalgo 110 (between Madero and Abasolo, 3½ blocks from the passenger-ferry pier), 77400 Isla Mujeres, Q. Roo. ⓒ 998/877-0430. Fax 998/877-0429. www.rolandi.com. 11 units. High season $56–$95 (£31–£52) double; low season $35–$95 (£19–£52) double. AE, MC, V. **Amenities:** Restaurant/bar (see "Where to Dine," below); room service; laundry service. *In room:* A/C, TV, fan.

Hotel D'Gomar *Value*   This hotel is known for comfort at reasonable prices. You can't beat the value for basic accommodations, which are regularly updated. Rooms have two double beds and a wall of windows—thus great breezes and views. The higher prices are for air-conditioning, which is hardly needed with the breezes and ceiling fans. The only drawback is that there are four stories and no elevator. But it's conveniently located cater-cornered (look right) from the ferry pier, with exceptional rooftop views. The name of the hotel is the most visible sign on the "skyline."

Rueda Medina 150, 77400 Isla Mujeres, Q. Roo. ℂ/fax **998/877-0541**. www.hotel dgomar.com. 16 units. High season $55–$65 (£30–£36) double; low season $50–$60 (£28–£33) double. MC, V. *In room:* A/C (in some), fan.

Hotel Francis Arlene ⋆

The Magaña family operates this neat little two-story inn built around a small, shady courtyard. This hotel is very popular with families and seniors, and it welcomes many repeat guests. You'll notice the tidy cream-and-white facade from the street. Some rooms have ocean views, and all are remodeled or updated each year. They are comfortable, with tile floors, tiled bathrooms, and a very homey feel. Each downstairs room has a coffeemaker, refrigerator, and stove; each upstairs room comes with a refrigerator and toaster. Some have either a balcony or a patio. Higher prices are for the 14 rooms with air-conditioning; other units have fans. Rates are substantially better if quoted in pesos; in dollars they are 15% to 20% higher.

Guerrero 7 (5½ blocks inland from the ferry pier, between Abasolo and Matamoros), 77400 Isla Mujeres, Q. Roo. ℂ/fax **998/877-0310** or -0861. www.francisarlene. com. 26 units. High season $55–$85 (£30–£47) double; low season $45–$65 (£25–£36) double. MC, V. **Amenities:** Safe; currency exchange. *In room:* A/C (in some), kitchenettes (in some), fridge, no phone.

Hotel Posada del Mar *(Kids)*

Simply furnished, quiet, and comfortable, this long-established hotel faces the water and a wide beach 3 blocks north of the ferry pier. This is probably the best choice in Isla for families. For the spaciousness of the rooms (half of which have ocean views) and the location, it's also among the island's best values. A wide, appealing but seldom-used stretch of Playa Norte lies across the street, where watersports equipment is available for rent. A great, casual *palapa*-style bar and a lovely pool are on the back lawn along with hammocks, and the restaurant **Pinguinos** (see "Where to Dine," below) is by the sidewalk at the front of the property, and also provides room service to hotel guests.

Av. Rueda Medina 15 A, 77400 Isla Mujeres, Q. Roo. ℂ **800/544-3005** in the U.S., or 998/877-0044. Fax 998/877-0266. www.posadadelmar.com. 52 units. High season $100 (£55) double; low season $60 (£33) double. Children younger than 12 stay free in parent's room. AE, MC, V. **Amenities:** Restaurant/bar; outdoor pool. *In room:* A/C, TV, fan.

WHERE TO DINE

At the **Municipal Market,** next to the telegraph office and post office on Avenida Guerrero, obliging, hardworking women operate several little food stands. At the **Panadería La Reyna** (no phone), at Madero and Juárez, you can pick up inexpensive sweet bread, muffins, cookies, and yogurt. It's open Monday through Saturday from 7am to 9:30pm.

Cocina económica (literally, "economical cuisine") restaurants usually aim at the local population. These are great places to find good food at rock-bottom prices, and especially so on Isla Mujeres, where you'll find several, most of which feature delicious regional specialties. But be aware that the hygiene is not what you'll find at more established restaurants, so you're dining at your own risk.

EXPENSIVE

Casa Rolandi ⭐ SWISS/ITALIAN   The gourmet Casa Rolandi restaurant and bar has become Isla's favored fine-dining experience. It boasts a wonderful view of the Caribbean and the most sophisticated menu in the area. There's a colorful main dining area as well as a more casual, open-air terrace. The food is the most notable on the island. Along with fresh fish, seafood, and northern Italian specialties, the famed wood-burning-oven pizzas are delicious. Careful—the wood-oven-baked bread, which arrives looking like a puffer fish—is so divine that you're likely to fill up on it. This is a great place to enjoy the sunset, and it offers a selection of fine international wines and more than 80 premium tequilas. Service is personalized and attentive.

On the pier of Villa Rolandi, Lagunamar SM 7. © **998/877-0700.** Main courses $8–$35 (£4.40–£19). AE, MC, V. Daily noon–11pm.

MODERATE

Angelo ⭐ ITALIAN   An authentic Italian restaurant in the pedestrian-friendly town center, Angelo offers an enticing selection of antipasti, pastas, grilled seafood, and wood-oven-baked pizzas. The Sardinian-born owner instills his menu with the flavors of his homeland, including a rich tomato sauce. Consider starting with a bowl of seafood soup or black mussels *au gratin* and continuing with the grilled shrimp kabobs or seafood pasta in an olive oil and white-wine sauce. The open-air restaurant includes an inviting sidewalk terrace and lies across the street from a casual Cuban restaurant also owned by Angelo.

Av. Hidalgo 14 (between Lopez Mateos and Matamoros). © **998/877-1273.** Main courses $6.50–$12 (£3.60–£6.60). MC, V. Daily 4pm–midnight.

Pinguinos MEXICAN/SEAFOOD   The best seats on the water-front stretch across the deck of this open-air restaurant and bar. Come late evening, islanders and tourists arrive to dance and party. This is the place to feast on sublimely fresh lobster—you'll get a large, beautifully presented lobster tail with a choice of butter, garlic, and secret sauces. The grilled seafood platter, seafood casserole, and fajitas are all spectacular. Breakfasts include fresh fruit, yogurt, and granola, or sizable platters of eggs, served with homemade wheat bread.

In front of the Hotel Posada del Mar (3 blocks west of the ferry pier), Av. Rueda Medina 15. © 998/877-0044, ext. 157. Breakfast $1.50–$7.50 (85p–£4.15); main courses $4.50–$17 (£2.50–£9.35). AE, MC, V. Daily 7am–11pm; bar closes at midnight.

Pizza Rolandi ★★ ITALIAN/SEAFOOD   You're bound to dine at least once at Rolandi's, which is practically an Isla institution. The plate-size pizzas and calzones feature exotic ingredients—including lobster, black mushrooms, pineapple, and Roquefort cheese—as well as more traditional tomatoes, olives, basil, and salami. A wood-burning oven provides the signature flavor of the pizzas, as well as baked chicken, roast beef, and mixed seafood casserole with lobster. The extensive menu also offers a selection of salads and light appetizers, as well as an ample array of flavorful homemade pasta dishes, steaks, fish, and scrumptious desserts. The setting is the open courtyard of the Hotel Belmar, with a porch overlooking the action on Avenida Hidalgo.

Av. Hidalgo 10 (3½ blocks inland from the pier, between Madero and Abasolo). © 998/877-0430, ext. 18. Main courses $7–$16 (£3.85–£8.80). AE, MC, V. Daily 11am–11:15pm.

Zazil Ha ★★ CARIBBEAN/INTERNATIONAL   Here you can enjoy some of the island's best food while sitting at tables on the sand among palms and gardens. Come night, candlelit tables sparkle underneath the open-air *palapa*. Specialties include Maya chicken stuffed with corn mushroom and goat cheese, black pasta with squid rings and pesto sauce, and fish of the day with *achiote* sauce draped in a banana leaf. A selection of fresh juices complements the vegetarian options, and there's even a special menu for those participating in yoga retreats. The delicious breads are baked in-house. Between the set meal times, you can order all sorts of enticing food, such as tacos and sandwiches, *ceviche,* terrific nachos, and vegetable and fruit drinks.

At the Hotel Na Balam (at the end of Playa Norte, almost at the end of Calle Zazil Ha). © 998/877-0279. Fax 998/877-0446. Breakfast $3.50–$9.50 (£1.95–£5.25); main courses $8.50–$22 (£4.70–£12). AE, MC, V. Daily 7:30am–10:30pm.

INEXPENSIVE

Café Cito 𝒦 CREPES/ICE CREAM/COFFEE/FRUIT DRINKS
Brisa and Luis Rivera own this adorable, Caribbean-blue corner restaurant where you can begin the day with flavorful coffee and a croissant and cream cheese (it's the only place in town where you can have breakfast until 2pm), or end it with a hot-fudge sundae. Terrific crepes come with yogurt, ice cream, fresh fruit, or *dulce de leche* (similar to caramel, but made with goat's milk) sauce, as well as ham and cheese. The two-page ice-cream menu satisfies almost any craving, even one for waffles with ice cream and fruit. The three-course fixed-price dinner includes soup, a main course (such as fish or curried shrimp with rice and salad), and dessert.

Calle Matamoros 42, at Juárez (4 blocks from the pier). ℰ **998/877-1470.** Crepes $3–$6 (£1.65–£3.30); breakfast $3.50–$5.50 (£1.95–£3); sandwiches $3.50–$4.50 (£1.95–£2.50). No credit cards. Daily 8am–2pm; high season Fri–Wed 5:30pm–10:30 or 11:30pm.

ISLA MUJERES AFTER DARK

Those in a party mood by day's end may want to start out at the beach bar of the **Na Balam** hotel on Playa Norte, which usually hosts a crowd until around midnight. On Saturday and Sunday, live music plays between 4 and 7pm. **Jax Bar & Grill** on Avenida Ruedo Medina, close to Hotel Posada del Mar, is a Texas-style sports bar offering live music nightly. **Las Palapas Chimbo's** restaurant on the beach becomes a jammin' dance joint with a live band from 9pm until whenever. Farther along the same stretch of beach, **Buho's,** the restaurant/beach bar of the Cabañas María del Mar, has its moments as a popular, low-key hangout, complete with swinging seats over the sand! **Pinguinos** in the Hotel Posada del Mar offers a convivial late-night hangout, where a band plays nightly during high season from 9pm to midnight. If you want to sample one of nearly 100 tequila brands on a relaxing sidewalk terrace, stop by **La Adelita,** located at Av. Hidalgo 12 and open nightly from 5:30pm to 2:30am. Near Matamoros and Hidalgo, **KoKo Nuts** caters to a younger crowd, with international music for late-night dancing. **Om Bar and Chill Lounge,** on Calle Matamoros, serves cocktails in an atmosphere that includes jazzy Latino music, open from 6pm to 2am. For a late night dance club, **Club Nitrox,** on Avenida Guererro, is open Wednesday to Sunday from 9pm to 3am. In general, the crowds hitting these bars are in their 20s.

2 Eco Theme Parks & Reserves

AKTUN CHEN ⟨⟨

Before you get to Xel-Ha (shell-*hah*) nature park, you'll pass the turnoff for **Aktun Chen** ⟨⟨ cavern (a bit beyond Akumal). Of the several caverns that I've toured in the Yucatán, this is one of the best—it has lots of geological features, good lighting, several underground pools, and large chambers, all carefully preserved. The tour takes about an hour and requires a good amount of walking, but the footing is good. You exit not far from where you enter. There is also a zoo with specimens of the local fauna. Some of the critters are allowed to run about freely. In my opinion, the cost of admission is high—$17 (£9.35) for adults, $9 (£4.95) for children—but this is true of several attractions on this coast. The cavern is open 9am to 5pm daily. The turnoff is to the right, and the cave is about 4km (2½ miles) from the road.

XCARET: A DEVELOPED NATURE PARK

A billboard in the airport of faraway Guadalajara reads in Spanish "And when visiting Xcaret, don't forget to enjoy the pleasures of the Riviera Maya, too." An exaggeration, but its point is well taken: Xcaret (pronounced "eesh-ca-*ret*") is the biggest attraction in these parts and is practically a destination unto itself. It even has its own resort (not recommended). If you're coming to these shores to avoid crowds, avoid this place. If you're here for entertainment and activities, you should consider visiting Xcaret. What Xcaret does, it does very well, and that is to present in one package a little bit of everything that the Yucatán (and the rest of Mexico for that matter) has to offer.

Think of the activities that people come to the Yucatán for: hanging out on the beach, scuba and snorkeling, cavern diving, visiting ruins, taking a siesta in a hammock under a grove of palm trees, hiking through tropical forest, meeting native Maya peoples—Xcaret has all that plus handicraft exhibitions; a bat cave; a butterfly pavilion; mushroom and orchid nurseries; and lots of wildlife on display, including native jaguars, manatees, sea turtles, monkeys, macaws, flamingos, and a petting aquarium. Children love it. What probably receives most of the comments is the underground river (a natural feature of the park and common in much of the Yucatán) that's been opened in places to allow snorkelers to paddle along with the current. What else? A number of tours and shows, including *charros*

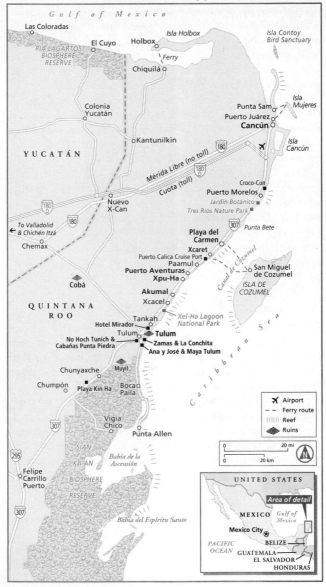

The Yucatán's Upper Caribbean Coast

Gulf of Mexico

Las Coloradas

Isla Holbox

El Cuyo
Holbox
Ferry

Isla Contoy
Bird Sanctuary

RÍA LAGARTOS
BIOSPHERE
RESERVE

Chiquilá

Colonia
Yucatán

Punta Sam
Isla
Mujeres
Puerto Juárez
Cancún

YUCATÁN

Kantunilkin

Isla
Cancún

180

Mérida Libre (no toll)

180
D

Cuota (toll)

Croco-Cun
Puerto Morelos

Nuevo
X-Can

Jardín Botánico
Tres Rios Nature Park

180
D

180

To Valladolid
& Chichén Itzá

**Playa del
Carmen**

Punta Bete

Chemax

Xcaret

Puerto Calica Cruise Port
Paamul
Puerto Aventuras
Xpu-Ha

San Miguel
de Cozumel

ISLA DE
COZUMEL

Cobá

Akumal

Xcacel

QUINTANA
ROO

Tankah

Xel-Ha Lagoon
National Park

Hotel Mirador
Tulum
No Hoch Tunich &
Cabañas Punta Piedra

Tulum
Zamas & La Conchita
Ana y José & Maya Tulum

Chunyaxche
Muyil

Chumpón
Playa Kin Ha
Boca
Paila

Caribbean Sea

Vigia
Chico

Punta Allen

295

Félipe
Carrillo
Puerto

SIAN
KA'AN
BIOSPHERE
RESERVE

Bahía de la
Ascensión

307

Bahía del Espíritu Santo

✈ Airport
- - - Ferry route
|||| Reef
◆ Ruins

0   20 mi
0   20 km

N

UNITED STATES

Area of detail

MEXICO

Gulf of
Mexico

Mexico City ⊗

BELIZE

PACIFIC
OCEAN

GUATEMALA
EL SALVADOR
HONDURAS

(Mexican cowboys) from the state of Jalisco, and the Totonac Indian *voladores* ("flyers" who do a daring pole dance high above the ground) from the state of Veracruz.

The park is famous for its evening spectacle that is a celebration of the Mexican nation. I've seen it and have to say that it is some show, with a large cast and lots of props. It starts with the Maya and an interpretation of how they may have played the pre-Hispanic game/ritual known as *pok-ta-pok*, and then to another version of a ballgame still practiced in the western state of Michoacán. From there it moves on to the arrival of the Spanish and eventually to the forging of the new nation and its customs.

Xcaret is 10km (6½ miles) south of Playa del Carmen (you'll know when you get to the turnoff). It's open daily from 8:30am to 9pm. Admission prices are $59 (£32) for adults, $41 (£23) for children 5 to 12. Certain activities cost extra: horseback ride $30 (£17), snuba/sea trek/snorkel tour $45 (£25), scuba $50 to $75 (£28–£41), swimming with dolphins $115 (£63). Other costs: lockers $2 (£1.10) per day, snorkel equipment $10 (£5.50) per day, food and drink variable. The park is an all-day affair; it's best to arrive early and register for tours and activities as soon as you can. For more info call © 998/883-3143 or visit www.xcaret.net.

XEL-HA 🐠🐠

Thirteen kilometers (8 miles) south of Akumal is **Xel-Ha** (© 998/ 884-9422 in Cancún, 984/873-3588 in Playa, or 984/875-6000 at the park; www.xelha.com.mx). The centerpiece of Xel-Ha is a large, beautiful lagoon where fresh water and salt water meet. You can swim, float, and snorkel in beautifully clear water surrounded by jungle. A small train takes guests upriver to a drop-off point. There, you can store all your clothes and gear in a locked sack that is taken down to the locker rooms in the main part of the building. The water moves calmly toward the sea, and you can float along with it. Snorkeling here offers a higher comfort level than the open sea— there are no waves and currents to pull you about, but there are a lot of fish of several species, including rays.

Inside the park, you can rent snorkeling equipment and an underwater camera. Platforms allow nonsnorkelers to view the fish. Another way to view fish is to use the park's snuba gear—a contraption that allows you to breathe air through 6m (20-ft.) tubes connected to scuba tanks floating on the surface. It frees you of the cumbersome tank while allowing you to stay down without having to hold your breath. Rental costs $45 (£25) for approximately an hour. Like snuba but more involved is sea-trek, a device consisting of an elaborate plastic helmet with air hoses. It allows you to walk around on the bottom breathing normally and perhaps participate in feeding the park's stingrays.

The park has completely remodeled and enlarged the dolphin area. This has improved the experience of swimming with these intelligent, powerful creatures. A 1-hour swim costs $115 (£63) plus park admission. You can also participate in a program that includes transportation from most hotels in the Riviera Maya and takes you to the dolphin area. It includes locker and equipment, too, all for $139 (£76). Make reservations (✆ **998/887-6840**) at least 24 hours in advance.

Other attractions include a plant nursery; an apiary for the local, stingerless Maya bees; and a lovely path through the tropical forest bordering the lagoon. Xel-Ha is open daily from 8:30am to 5pm. Parking is free. Admission is $33 (£18) adults, and $23 (£13) children ages 5 to 11; children younger than 5 enter free. Admission includes use of inner tubes, life vests, and shuttle train to the river, and the use of changing rooms and showers. (Though not listed on the website, the park often has discount admission during the weekend.) An all-inclusive option includes snorkeling equipment rental, locker rental, towels, food, and beverages. Adults can visit all week long for $59 (£32), and children visit for $41 (£23). These prices are not discounted on the weekend. The park has five restaurants, two ice-cream shops, and a store. It accepts American Express, MasterCard, and Visa, and it has an ATM.

Signs clearly mark the turnoff to Xel-Ha. Xel-Ha is close to the ruins of Tulum. A popular day tour from Cancún or Playa combines the two. If you're traveling on your own, the best time to enjoy Xel-Ha without the crowds is during the weekend from 9am to 2pm.

About 2km (1 mile) south of Xel-Ha are the **Hidden Worlds Cenotes** ★★★ (✆ **984/877-8535;** www.hiddenworlds.com.mx), which offers an excellent opportunity to snorkel or dive in a couple of nearby caverns. The caverns are part of a vast network that makes up a single underground river system. The water is crystalline (and cold) and the rock formations impressive. These caverns were filmed for the IMAX production *Journey into Amazing Caves.* The people running the show are resourceful. The snorkel tour costs $40 (£22) and takes you to two different caverns (a half tour costs $25/£14). The main form of transportation is "jungle mobile," with a guide who throws in tidbits of information and lore about local jungle plant life. There is some walking involved, so take shoes or sandals. I've toured several caverns, but floating through one gave me an entirely different perspective. For divers, a one-tank dive is $50 (£28), a two-tank experience is $90 (£50). The owners have also installed a 180m (590-ft.) zip-line on the property. I haven't tried it, but it looks fast.

3 Exploring the Punta Allen Peninsula

If you've been captured by an adventurous spirit and have an excessively sanguine opinion of your rental car's off-road capabilities, you might want to take a trip down the Punta Allen Peninsula, especially if your interests lie in fly-fishing, birding, or simply exploring new country. The far end of the peninsula is only 50km (30 miles) away, but it can be a very slow and bouncy trip (up to 3 hr., depending on the condition of the road). Not far from the last cabaña hotel is the entrance to the 500,000-hectare (1.3-million-acre) **Sian Ka'an Biosphere Reserve** (see below).

Halfway down the peninsula, at a small bridge, is the **Boca Paila Fishing Lodge** (www.bocapaila.com). Not for the general traveler, it specializes in hosting fly-fishers, with weeklong all-inclusive fishing packages. At this point, the peninsula is quite narrow. You can see the Boca Paila lagoon on one side and the sea on the other. Another 25km (15 miles) gets you to the village of Punta Allen. Before the town is a little hotel called **Rancho Sol Caribe.** It has only four rooms and a lovely beach all to itself. Punta Allen is a lobstering and fishing village on a palm-studded beach. Isolated and rustic, it's very much the laid-back end of the line. It has a lobster cooperative, a few streets with modest homes, and a lighthouse. The **Cuzan Guesthouse** (www.flyfishmx.com) is a collection of 12 cabins and one restaurant on a nice sandy beach. Its main clientele is fly-fishers, and it offers all-inclusive fishing packages. But co-owner Sonia Litvak, a Californian, will rent to anyone curious enough to want to go down there. She also offers snorkeling trips and boat tours.

THE SIAN KA'AN BIOSPHERE RESERVE

Down the peninsula a few miles south of the Tulum ruins, you'll pass the guardhouse of the Sian Ka'an Biosphere Reserve. The reserve is a tract of 500,000 hectares (1.3 million acres) set aside in 1986 to preserve tropical forests, savannas, mangroves, coastal and marine habitats, and 110km (70 miles) of coastal reefs. The area is home to jaguars; pumas; ocelots; margays; jaguarundis; spider and howler monkeys; tapirs; white-lipped and collared peccaries; manatees; brocket and white-tailed deer; crocodiles; and green, loggerhead, hawksbill, and leatherback sea turtles. It also protects 366 species of birds—you might catch a glimpse of an ocellated turkey, a great curassow, a brilliantly colored parrot, a toucan or trogon, a white ibis, a roseate spoonbill, a jabiru (or wood stork), a flamingo, or one of 15 species of herons, egrets, and bitterns.

The park has three parts: a "core zone" restricted to research; a "buffer zone," to which visitors and families already living there have restricted use; and a "cooperation zone," which is outside the reserve but vital to its preservation. There are two principal entrances to the biosphere reserve: one is from the community of Muyil, which is off Highway 307, south of Tulum (you take a boat down canals built by the Maya that connect to the Boca Paila lagoon); the other is from the community of Punta Allen (by jeep down the peninsula, which separates the Boca Paila Lagoon from the sea).

Visitors can arrange day trips in Tulum from a few different outfits, whose offices are just a couple of blocks apart and even have similar names. **Sian Ka'an Tours** (© **984/871-2363;** siankaan_tours@hotmail.com) is on the west side of Avenida Tulum, next to El Basilico Restaurant, at the corner of Calle Beta. **Community Tours Sian Ka'an** is on the same side of the road, 2 blocks north between Orion and Centauro streets (© **984/114-0750;** www.siankaantours.org). The latter is a community organization of Muyil and Punta Allen. Both will pick up customers from any of the area hotels.

5

A Glimpse of the Maya: Nearby Ruins

Despite Cancún's bounty of diversions, the region surrounding the beach resort is even richer in natural and cultural pleasures. Those who bemoan the rather Americanized ways of Cancún will find compensation in the Yucatán's more authentic experience and relaxed charm. With a little exploring, you'll find a variety of things to do. This chapter covers the best-known Maya ruins of the Yucatán Peninsula, including the seaside ruins of **Tulum,** the jungle complex at **Cobá,** and the supremely restored site at **Chichén Itzá.** These treasures are at once close to the easy air access of Cancún, yet miles away in mood and manner.

EXPLORING THE YUCATAN'S MAYA HEARTLAND

The best way to see the Yucatán is by car. The terrain is flat, there is little traffic once you get away from the cities, and the main highways are in good shape. If you drive at all around this area, you will add at least one new word to your Spanish vocabulary—*topes* (*toh-pehs*), meaning speed bumps. And along with *topes* you might learn a few new curse words. *Topes* come in varying shapes and sizes and with varying degrees of warning. Don't let them surprise you.

Off the main highways, the roads are narrow and rough, but hey—you'll be driving a rental car. Rentals are, in fact, a little pricey compared with those in the U.S. (due perhaps to wear and tear?), but some promotional deals are available, especially in low season. Plenty of buses ply the roads between the major towns and ruins. And plenty of tour buses circulate, too. But buses to the smaller towns and ruins and the haciendas are infrequent. One bus company, Autobuses del Oriente (ADO), controls most of the first-class bus service and does a good job with the major destinations. Second-class buses go to some out-of-the-way places, but they can be slow, stop a lot, and usually aren't air-conditioned. I will take them when going short distances. If you don't want to rent a car, a few tour operators take small groups to more remote attractions such as ruins, *cenotes,* and villages.

The Yucatán is *tierra caliente* (the hot lands). Don't travel in this region without a hat, sunblock, mosquito repellent, and water. The coolest weather is from November to February; the hottest is from April to June. From July to October, thundershowers moderate temperatures. More tourists come to the interior during the winter months, but not to the same extent as on the Caribbean coast. The high-season/low-season distinction is less pronounced here.

1 Tulum

The Tulum ruins are a walled Maya city of the post-Classic age perched on a rocky cliff overlooking the Caribbean. Tulum beach used to be a destination for backpackers, but the *palapa* hotels have gone upscale, and the beach now attracts a well-heeled crowd that seeks to get away from the bustle of the big hotels and resorts. The town of Tulum has several modest hotels, more than a dozen restaurants, several stores and pharmacies, three cybercafes, a few dive shops, a bank, two ATMs, and a new bus station.

ESSENTIALS
GETTING THERE
Drive south from Cancún on Highway 307. The ruins are 130km (81 miles) southwest of Cancún.

ORIENTATION
To visit the Tulum area, get a rental car; it will make everything much easier. Coming from the north you'll pass the entrance to the ruins before arriving at the town. You'll come to a highway intersection with a traffic light. To the right is the highway leading to the ruins of Cobá (see "Cobá Ruins," later in this chapter); to the left is the Tulum hotel zone, which begins about 2km (1½ miles) away. The road sign reads BOCA PAILA, which is a place halfway down the **Punta Allen Peninsula.** This road eventually goes all the way to the tip of the peninsula and the town of Punta Allen, a lobstering and fishing village. It is a rough road that is slow going for most of the way. A few kilometers down the road, you will enter the **Biosphere Reserve.**

The town of Tulum is growing quickly. It now extends for 3 or more blocks in either direction from the highway. The highway widens here and is called Avenida Tulum. It is lined with stores, restaurants, and the offices of service providers. One place that I find handy to visit is a travel agency/communications/package center called **Savana** (© **984/871-2081**) on the east side of Avenida Tulum between calles Orion and Beta. The staff, for the most part, speaks English and can answer questions about tours and calling home.

EXPLORING THE TULUM ARCHAEOLOGICAL SITE

Thirteen kilometers (8 miles) south of Xel-Ha are the ruins of Tulum, a Maya fortress-city on a cliff above the sea. The ruins are open to visitors daily from 7am to 5pm in the winter, 8am to 6pm in the summer. It's always best to go early, before the crowds start showing up (around 9:30am). The entrance to the ruins is about a 5-minute walk from the archaeological site. There are artisans' stands, a bookstore, a museum, a restaurant, several large bathrooms, and a ticket booth. Admission fee to the ruins is $4 (£2.20). If you want to ride the shuttle from the visitor center to the ruins, it's another $1.50 (85p). Parking is $3 (£1.65). A video camera permit costs $4 (£2.20). Licensed guides have a stand next to the path to the ruins and charge $20 (£11) for a 45-minute tour in English, French, or Spanish for up to four persons. In some ways, they are like performers and will tailor their presentation to the responses they receive from you. Some will try to draw connections between the Maya and Western theology, and they will point out architectural details that you might otherwise miss.

By A.D. 900, the end of the Classic period, Maya civilization had begun its decline, and the large cities to the south were abandoned. Tulum is one of the small city-states that rose to fill the void. It came to prominence in the 13th century as a seaport, controlling maritime commerce along this section of the coast, and remained inhabited well after the arrival of the Spanish. The primary god here was the diving god, depicted on several buildings as an upside-down figure above doorways. Seen at the Palace at Sayil and Cobá, this curious, almost comical figure is also known as the bee god.

The most imposing building in Tulum is a large stone structure above the cliff called the **Castillo** (castle). Actually a temple as well as a fortress, it was once covered with stucco and painted. In front of the Castillo are several unrestored palacelike buildings partially covered with stucco. On the **beach** below, where the Maya once came ashore, tourists swim and sunbathe, combining a visit to the ruins with a dip in the Caribbean.

The **Temple of the Frescoes,** directly in front of the Castillo, contains interesting 13th-century wall paintings, though entrance is

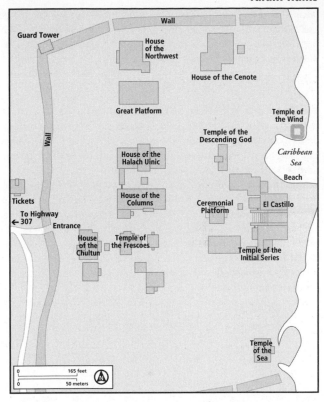

no longer permitted. Distinctly Maya, they represent the rain god Chaac, and Ixchel, the goddess of weaving, women, the moon, and medicine. On the cornice of this temple is a relief of the head of the rain god. If you pause a slight distance from the building, you'll see the eyes, nose, mouth, and chin. Notice the remains of the red-painted stucco—at one time all the buildings at Tulum were painted bright red.

Much of what we know of Tulum at the time of the Spanish Conquest comes from the writings of Diego de Landa, third bishop of the Yucatán. He wrote that Tulum was a small city inhabited by about 600 people who lived in platform dwellings along a street and who supervised the trade traffic from Honduras to the Yucatán. Though it was a walled city, most of the inhabitants probably lived outside the walls, leaving the interior for the residences of governors and priests and ceremonial structures. Tulum survived about 70 years after the conquest, when it was finally abandoned. Because of the great number of visitors this site receives, it is no longer possible to climb all of the ruins. In many cases, visitors are asked to remain behind roped-off areas to view them.

WHERE TO STAY IN & AROUND TULUM

If you can afford staying at one of the small beach hotels in Tulum, do so. The experience is enjoyable and relaxing. But most are on the expensive side. Demand is high, supply is limited, and the hotels have to generate their own electricity (bring a flashlight). Most of the inexpensive hotels are not that comfortable. If you're on a budget, you will be more comfortable staying in Akumal or in one of the modest hotels in town and be a day-tripper to the beach.

Take the Boca Paila road from Highway 307. Three kilometers (2 miles) ahead, you come to a T-junction. To the south are most of the *palapa* hotels; to the north are several, too. The rates listed below don't include the week of Christmas and New Year, when prices go above regular high-season rates.

VERY EXPENSIVE

Ana y José 🐟🐟 This *palapa* hotel has gone "boutique" with a spa, suites, and serious remodeling of rooms. It's a far cry now from what it used to be—a simple collection of cabins and a restaurant on the beach. Now there are marble countertops and marble tile floors. Rooms are large and comfortable. There's A/C in all the lower rooms that don't catch the sea breeze. The two beachfront rock cabins in front of the property have remained unchanged and are a little lower in price than the other beachfront and oceanview rooms. The beach here is excellent. Ana y José is 6.5km (4 miles) south of the Tulum ruins.

Carretera Punta Allen Km 7 (Apdo. Postal 15), 77780 Tulum, Q. Roo. ✆ **998/887-5470.** Fax 998/887-5469. www.anayjose.com. 22 units. $233–$255 (£128–£140) garden and pool view; $306–$373 (£168–£205) beachfront and ocean view. AE, MC, V. Free parking. **Amenities:** Restaurant; outdoor pool; spa; tour info; car rental. *In room:* A/C in some rooms, safe, no phone.

Azulik 🐟🐟 Azulik is all about slowing down, leaving civilization behind (except for such niceties as indoor plumbing and room service), and enjoying the simple life (with or without clothes). I enjoyed the simple life during an all-too-brief stay here, and what I liked most about Azulik was the design and positioning of the individual

cabañas. All but three of them sit on a stone ledge next to, and a little above, the sea. The ledge is just high enough to provide privacy
while you sit out on the semi-shaded wood deck in front of your
cabaña enjoying either the sun or the stars. For that purpose, they
come with chairs, hammocks, and a wooden tub for soaking. (There
is a larger wooden tub indoors for bathing.) Each cabaña is constructed entirely of wood and glass and thatch. There is no electricity,
only candles. Each has a king-size bed with mosquito netting and a
queen-size bed, suspended on ropes, for lounging during the day. This
property shares a good restaurant and a good spa with a sister hotel.

Carretera Boca Paila Km 5.5, 77780 Tulum, Q. Roo. ℭ 877/532-6737 in the U.S.
and Canada. www.azulik.com. 15 units. High season $240–$260 (£132–£143) double; low season $190–$210 (£105–£116) double, MC, V. Limited free parking. Children younger than 18 not accepted. **Amenities:** Restaurant; bar; spa; room service.
In room: Safe, no phone.

MODERATE

Posada Dos Ceibas *☆*   Of all the places along this coast, this one
reminds me the most of the way hotels in Tulum used to be. Simple, quiet, and ecological without being pretentious. This is a good
choice for a no-fuss beach vacation. The one- and two-story cottages
are spread out through the vegetation. Rooms are simply furnished
and come with ceiling fans, and almost all have private patios or
porches. Price varies according to the size of the rooms. The grounds
are well tended. The electricity is solar generated and comes on at
6pm. There is a pure sand beach.

Carretera Tulum-Boca Paila Km 10, 77780 Tulum, Q. Roo. ℭ 984/877-6024.
www.dosceibas.com. 8 units. High season $100–$220 (£55–£121) double; low season $75–$145 (£41–£80) double. MC, V. **Amenities:** Restaurant; massage; yoga
classes. *In room:* No phone.

Zamas *☆☆*   The owners of these cabañas, a couple from San Francisco, have made their rustic getaway most enjoyable by concentrat-
ing on the essentials: comfort, privacy, and good food. The cabañas
are simple, attractive, well situated for catching the breeze, and not
too close together. Most rooms are in individual structures; the suites
and oversize rooms are in modest two-story buildings. For the
money, I like the individual garden *palapas,* which are attractive, spacious, and comfortable, and come with a queen-size bed and a twin
or a king- and queen-size bed. Two small beachfront cabañas with
one queen-size bed go for a little less. The most expensive rooms are
the upstairs oceanview units, which enjoy a large terrace and lots of
sea breezes. They come with a king-size and a queen-size bed or two

queen-size beds. The restaurant serves the freshest seafood—I've actually seen the owner flag down passing fishermen to buy their catch. A white-sand beach stretches between large rocky areas.

Carretera Punta Allen Km 5, 77780 Tulum, Q. Roo. © 415/387-9806 in the U.S. www.zamas.com. 20 units. High season $105–$150 (£58–£83) beachfront double, $110–$135 (£61–£74) garden double, $180 (£99) oceanview double; low season $85–$95 (£47–£52) beachfront double, $80–$115 (£44–£63) garden double, $135 (£74) oceanview double. No credit cards. Limited free parking. **Amenities:** Restaurant. *In room:* No phone.

INEXPENSIVE

Cabañas Tulum   Next to Ana y José is a row of cinder-block bungalows facing the same beautiful ocean and beach. Rooms are simple and poorly lit, with basic bathrooms. All rooms have two double beds (most with new mattresses), screens on the windows, a table, one electric light, and a porch facing the beach. Electricity is available from 7 to 11am and 5 to 11pm.

Carretera Punta Allen Km 7 (Apdo. Postal 63), 77780 Tulum, Q. Roo. © 984/879-7395. Fax 984/871-2092. www.hotelstulum.com. 32 units. $60–$80 (£33–£44) double. No credit cards. Limited free parking. **Amenities:** Restaurant; game room. *In room:* No phone.

WHERE TO DINE

There are several restaurants in the town of Tulum. They are reasonably priced and do an okay job. On the main street are **Charlie's** (© 984/871-2136), my favorite for Mexican food, and **Don Cafeto's** (© 984/871-2207). A good Italian-owned Italian restaurant, **Il Giardino** (© 984/804-1316; closed Wed), is a block off the highway on the town's northernmost cross street, Satelite. At **Azafrán** (© 984/129-6130) you can get amazingly sophisticated cooking served in a small, rustic dining room. Also in town are a couple of roadside places that grill chicken and serve it with rice and beans. And there's a local people's restaurant at the southern end of town called **Doña Tina.** Meals on the coast are going to be more expensive but more varied. Many of the hotels have restaurants—I've eaten well at **Copal** and **Mezzanine,** which are both north of the T-junction, and **Zamas,** which is south.

2 Cobá Ruins

Older than most of Chichén Itzá and much larger than Tulum, Cobá was the dominant city of the eastern Yucatán before A.D. 1000. The site is large and spread out, with thick forest growing between the temple groups. Rising high above the forest canopy are

tall and steep pyramids of the Classic Maya style. Of the major sites, this one is the least reconstructed and so disappoints those who expect another Chichén Itzá. The stone sculpture here has worn off and has become impossible to make out. But the structures themselves and the surrounding jungle and twin lakes make the experience enjoyable. This is not a *cenote* area, and the water has nowhere to go but stay on the surface. The forest canopy is also higher than in the northern part of the peninsula.

ESSENTIALS

GETTING THERE & DEPARTING   By Car   The road to Cobá begins in Tulum and continues for 65km (40 miles). Watch out for both *topes* (speed bumps) and potholes. The road is going to be repaved and widened this year. Close to the village of Cobá you will come to a triangle offering you three choices: Nuevo Xcan, Valladolid, and Cobá. Make sure not to get on the other two roads. The entrance to the ruins is a short distance down the road past some small restaurants and the large lake.

By Bus   Several buses a day leave Tulum and Playa del Carmen for Cobá. Several companies offer bus tours.

EXPLORING THE COBA RUINS

The Maya built many intriguing cities in the Yucatán, but few grander than Cobá ("water stirred by wind"). Much of the 67-sq.-km (26-sq.-mile) site remains unexcavated. A 100km (62-mile) *sacbé* (a pre-Hispanic raised road or causeway) through the jungle linked Cobá to Yaxuná, once an important Maya center 50km (30 miles) south of Chichén Itzá. It's the Maya's longest known *sacbé*, and at least 50 shorter ones lead from here. An important city-state,

Cobá flourished from A.D. 632 (the oldest carved date found here) until after the rise of Chichén Itzá, around 800. Then Cobá slowly faded in importance and population until it was finally abandoned. Scholars believe Cobá was an important trade link between the Yucatán Caribbean coast and inland cities.

Once at the site, keep your bearings—you can get turned around in the maze of dirt roads in the jungle. And bring bug spray. As spread out as this city is, renting a bike (which you can do at the entrance for $2.50/£1.40) is a good option. Branching off from every labeled path, you'll notice unofficial narrow paths into the jungle, used by locals as shortcuts through the ruins. These are good for birding, but be careful to remember the way back.

The **Grupo Cobá** holds an impressive pyramid, **La Iglesia (the Temple of the Church),** which you'll find if you take the path bearing right after the entrance. Though the urge to climb the temple is great, the view is better from El Castillo in the Nohoch Mul group farther back.

From here, return to the main path and turn right. You'll pass a sign pointing right to the ruined *juego de pelota* **(ball court),** but the path is obscure.

Continuing straight ahead on this path for 5 to 10 minutes, you'll come to a fork in the road. To the left and right you'll notice jungle-covered, unexcavated pyramids, and at one point, you'll see a raised portion crossing the pathway—this is the visible remains of the *sacbé* to Yaxuná. Throughout the area, carved stelae stand by pathways or lie forlornly in the jungle underbrush. Although protected by crude thatched roofs, most are weatherworn enough that they're indiscernible.

The left fork leads to the **Nohoch Mul Group,** which contains **El Castillo.** With the exception of Structure 2 in Calakmul, this is the tallest pyramid in the Yucatán (rising even higher than the great El Castillo at Chichén Itzá and the Pyramid of the Magician at Uxmal). Visitors are permitted to climb to the top. From this lofty perch, you can see unexcavated jungle-covered pyramidal structures poking up through the forest canopy all around.

For Your Comfort at Cobá

Visit Cobá in the morning or after the heat of the day has passed. Mosquito repellent, drinking water, and comfortable shoes are imperative.

The right fork (more or less straight on) goes to the **Conjunto Las Pinturas.** Here, the main attraction is the **Pyramid of the Painted Lintel,** a small structure with traces of its original bright colors above the door. You can climb up to get a close look. Though maps of Cobá show ruins around two lakes, there are really only two excavated groups.

Admission is $4 (£2.20), free for children younger than age 12. Parking is $1 (55p). A video camera permit costs $4 (£2.20). The site is open daily from 8am to 5pm, sometimes longer.

WHERE TO STAY & DINE

If nightfall catches you in Cobá, you have limited lodging choices. There is one tourist hotel called **Villas Arqueológicas Cobá,** which fronts the lake and is operated by Club Med. Though smaller than its sister hotels in Uxmal and Chichén Itzá, it's the same in style— modern rooms that are attractive and functional, so long as you're not too tall. It has a restaurant that serves all three meals. It could be empty or full since most of its business comes from bus tours. To make reservations, call © **800/258-2633** in the U.S., or 55/ 5203-3086 in Mexico. It has a swimming pool. There's also a cheap hotel in town called **El Bocadito** (no phone) with simple rooms for $25 (£14) per night. It has a small restaurant, and there are a couple more in the town as well.

3 The Ruins of Chichén Itzá

The fabled ruins of Chichén Itzá (no, it doesn't rhyme with "chicken pizza"; the accents are on the last syllables: chee-*chen* eet-*zah*) are the Yucatán's best-known ancient monuments. They are plenty hyped, but Chichén merits a visit. Walking among these stone platforms, pyramids, and ball courts gives you an appreciation for this ancient civilization that books cannot convey. The city is built on a scale that evokes a sense of wonder: To fill the plazas during one of the mass rituals that occurred here a millennium ago would have required an enormous number of celebrants. Even today, with the mass flow of tourists through these plazas, the ruins feel empty.

When visiting the ruins, keep in mind that much of what is said about the Maya (especially by tour guides, who speak in tones of utter certainty) is merely educated guessing. This much we do know: The area was settled by farmers as far back as the 4th century A.D. The first signs of an urban society appear in the 7th century in the construction of stone temples and palaces in the traditional Puuc Maya style. These buildings can be found in the "Old Chichén" section of the city. Construction continued for a couple hundred years. In the 10th century (the post-Classic era), the city came under the rule of the Itzáes, who arrived from central Mexico by way of the Gulf Coast. They may have been a mix of highland Toltec Indians (the people who built the city of Tula in central Mexico) and lowland Putún Maya, who were a commercial people thriving on trade between the different regions of the area. In the following centuries, the city saw its greatest growth. Most of the grand architecture was built during this age in a style that is clearly Toltec influenced. The new rulers may have been refugees from Tula. There is a mythological story told in pre-Columbian central Mexico about a fight that occurred between the gods Quetzalcoatl and Tezcatlipoca, which resulted in Quetzalcoatl being forced to leave his homeland and venture east. This may be a shorthand account of a civil war in Tula, between different religious factions, with the losers fleeing to the Yucatán, where they were welcomed by the local Maya. Over time, the Itzáes adopted more and more the ways of the Maya. Sometime at the end of the 12th century, the city was captured by its rival, the city of Mayapán.

Though it's possible to make a day trip from Cancún or Mérida, it's preferable to overnight here or in nearby Valladolid. It makes for a more relaxing trip. You can see the light show in the evening and return to see the ruins early the next morning when it is cool and before the tour buses arrive.

ESSENTIALS

GETTING THERE & DEPARTING   By Plane   Travel agents in the United States, Cancún, and Cozumel can arrange day trips from Cancún and Cozumel.

By Car   Chichén Itzá is on old Highway 180 between Mérida and Cancún. The fastest way to get there from either city is to take the *autopista* (or *cuota*). The toll is $7 (£3.85) from Mérida, $22 (£12) from Cancún. Once you have exited the *autopista*, you will turn onto the road leading to the village of Pisté. Once in the village, you'll reach a T junction at Highway 180 and turn left to get to the ruins. The entrance to the ruins is well marked. If you stay on the highway for a few kilometers more you'll come to the exit for the hotel zone at Km 121 (before you reach the turnoff, you'll pass

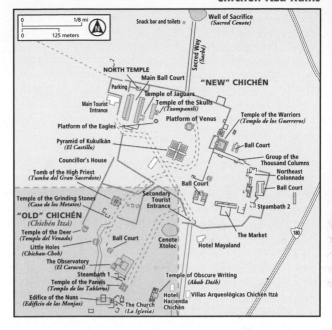

the eastern entrance to Mayapán, which is usually closed). Chichén is 1½ hours from Mérida and 2½ hours from Cancún.

By Bus   From Mérida, there are three first-class ADO buses per day. There are also a couple of first-class buses to Cancún and Playa. Otherwise, you can buy a second-class bus ticket to Valladolid and a first-class from there. If you want to take a day trip from Mérida or Cancún, go with a tour company.

AREA LAYOUT   The village of **Pisté,** where most of the economical hotels and restaurants are located, is about 2.5km (1½ miles) to the west of the ruins. Public buses can drop you off here. And located on the old highway 2.5km (1½ miles) east from the ruins is another economical hotel, the Hotel Dolores Alba (see "Where to Stay," below). Situated at the ruins of Chichén Itzá are three luxury hotels.

EXPLORING THE RUINS

The site occupies 6.5 sq. km (2½ sq. miles), and it takes most of a day to see all the ruins, which are open daily from 8am to 5pm. Service areas are open from 8am to 10pm. Admission is $10 (£5.50), free for children younger than age 12. A video camera permit costs $4 (£2.20). Parking is extra. **Note:** You can use your ticket to reenter on the same day. The cost of admission includes the **sound-and-light show,** which is worth seeing since you're being charged for it anyway. The show, held at 7 or 8pm depending on the season, is in Spanish, but headsets are available for rent in several languages. The narrative is okay, but the real reason for seeing the show is the lights, which show off the beautiful geometry of the city.

The large, modern visitor center, at the main entrance where you pay the admission charge, is beside the parking lot and consists of a museum, an auditorium, a restaurant, a bookstore, and bathrooms. You can see the site on your own or with a licensed guide who speaks English or Spanish. Guides usually wait at the entrance and charge around $45 (£25) for one to six people. Although the guides frown on it, there's nothing wrong with approaching a group of people who speak the same language and asking if they want to share a guide. These guides can point out architectural details often missed when visiting on your own. Chichén Itzá has two parts: the central (new) zone, which shows distinct Toltec influence, and the southern (old) zone, with mostly Puuc architecture.

EL CASTILLO As you enter from the tourist center, the magnificent 25m (82-ft.) El Castillo pyramid (also called the Pyramid of Kukulkán) will be straight ahead across a large open area. It was built with the Maya calendar in mind. The four stairways leading up to the central platform each have 91 steps, making a total of 364, which when you add the central platform equals the 365 days of the solar year. On either side of each stairway are nine terraces, which makes 18 on each face of the pyramid, equaling the number of months in the Maya solar calendar. On the facing of these terraces are 52 panels (we don't know how they were decorated), which represent the 52-year cycle when both the solar and religious calendars would become realigned. The pyramid's alignment is such that on the **spring** or **fall equinox** (Mar 21 or Sept 21) a curious event occurs. The setting sun casts the shadow of the terraces onto the ramp of the northern stairway. A diamond pattern is formed, suggestive of the geometric designs on some snakes. Slowly it descends into the earth. The effect is more conceptual than visual, and to view it requires being with a large crowd. It's much better to see the ruins on other days when it's less crowded.

El Castillo was built over an earlier structure. A narrow stairway at the western edge of the north staircase leads inside that structure, where there is a sacrificial altar-throne—a red jaguar encrusted with jade. The stairway is open from 11am to 3pm and is cramped, usually crowded, humid, and uncomfortable. A visit early in the day is best. Photos of the jaguar figure are not allowed.

JUEGO DE PELOTA (MAIN BALL COURT)   Northwest of El Castillo is Chichén's main ball court, the largest and best preserved anywhere, and only one of nine ball courts built in this city. Carved on both walls of the ball court are scenes showing Maya figures dressed as ballplayers and decked out in heavy protective padding. The carved scene also shows a headless player kneeling with blood shooting from his neck; another player holding the head looks on.

Players on two teams tried to knock a hard rubber ball through one of the two stone rings placed high on either wall, using only their elbows, knees, and hips. According to legend, the losing players paid for defeat with their lives. However, some experts say the victors were the only appropriate sacrifices for the gods. One can only guess what the incentive for winning might be in that case. Either way, the game must have been riveting, heightened by the wonderful acoustics of the ball court.

THE NORTH TEMPLE   Temples are at both ends of the ball court. The North Temple has sculptured pillars and more sculptures inside, as well as badly ruined murals. The acoustics of the ball court are so good that from the North Temple, a person speaking can be heard clearly at the opposite end, about 135m (443 ft.) away.

TEMPLE OF JAGUARS   Near the southeastern corner of the main ball court is a small temple with serpent columns and carved panels showing warriors and jaguars. Up the steps and inside the temple, a mural was found that chronicles a battle in a Maya village.

TZOMPANTLI (TEMPLE OF THE SKULLS)   To the right of the ball court is the Temple of the Skulls, an obvious borrowing from the post-Classic cities of central Mexico. Notice the rows of skulls carved into the stone platform. When a sacrificial victim's head was cut off, it was impaled on a pole and displayed in a tidy row with others. Also carved into the stone are pictures of eagles tearing hearts from human victims. The word *Tzompantli* is not Mayan but comes from central Mexico. Reconstruction using scattered fragments may add a level to this platform and change the look of this structure by the time you visit.

PLATFORM OF THE EAGLES   Next to the Tzompantli, this small platform has reliefs showing eagles and jaguars clutching human hearts in their talons and claws, as well as a human head emerging from the mouth of a serpent.

PLATFORM OF VENUS   East of the Tzompantli and north of El Castillo, near the road to the Sacred Cenote, is the Platform of Venus. In Maya and Toltec lore, a feathered monster or a feathered serpent with a human head in its mouth represented Venus. This is also called the tomb of Chaac-Mool because a Chaac-Mool figure was discovered "buried" within the structure.

SACRED CENOTE   Follow the dirt road (actually an ancient *sacbé,* or causeway) that heads north from the Platform of Venus; after 5 minutes you'll come to the great natural well that may have given Chichén Itzá (the Well of the Itzáes) its name. This well was used for ceremonial purposes. Sacrificial victims were thrown in. Anatomical research done early in the 20th century by Ernest A. Hooten showed that bones of both children and adults were found in the well.

Edward Thompson, who was the American consul in Mérida and a Harvard professor, purchased the ruins of Chichén early in the 20th century and explored the *cenote* with dredges and divers. His explorations exposed a fortune in gold and jade. Most of the riches wound up in Harvard's Peabody Museum of Archaeology and Ethnology—a matter that continues to disconcert Mexican classicists today. Excavations in the 1960s unearthed more treasure, and studies of the recovered objects detail offerings from throughout the Yucatán and even farther away.

TEMPLO DE LOS GUERREROS (TEMPLE OF THE WARRIORS)   Due east of El Castillo is one of the most impressive structures at Chichén: the Temple of the Warriors, named for the carvings of warriors marching along its walls. It's also called the Group of the Thousand Columns for the rows of broken pillars that flank it. During the recent restoration, hundreds more of the columns were rescued from the rubble and put in place, setting off the temple more magnificently than ever. A figure of Chaac-Mool sits at the top of the temple, surrounded by impressive columns carved in relief to look like enormous feathered serpents. South of the temple was a square building that archaeologists call **El Mercado (The Market);** a colonnade surrounds its central court. Beyond the temple and the market in the jungle are mounds of rubble, parts of which are being reconstructed.

The main Mérida-Cancún highway once ran straight through the ruins of Chichén, and though it has been diverted, you can still see the great swath it cut. South and west of the old highway's path are more impressive ruined buildings.

TUMBA DEL GRAN SACERDOTE (TOMB OF THE HIGH PRIEST)   Past the refreshment stand to the right of the path is the Tomb of the High Priest, which stood atop a natural limestone cave in which skeletons and offerings were found, giving the temple its name.

CASA DE LOS METATES (TEMPLE OF THE GRINDING STONES)   This building, the next one on your right, is named after the concave corn-grinding stones the Maya used.

TEMPLO DEL VENADO (TEMPLE OF THE DEER)   Past Casa de los Metates is this fairly tall though ruined building. The relief of a stag that gave the temple its name is long gone.

CHICHANCHOB (LITTLE HOLES)   This next temple has a roof comb with little holes, three masks of the rain god Chaac, three rooms, and a good view of the surrounding structures. It's one of the oldest buildings at Chichén, built in the Puuc style during the late Classic period.

EL CARACOL (OBSERVATORY)   Construction of the Observatory, a complex building with a circular tower, was carried out over centuries; the additions and modifications reflected the Maya's careful observation of celestial movements and their need for increasingly exact measurements. Through slits in the tower's walls, astronomers could observe the cardinal directions and the approach of the all-important spring and autumn equinoxes, as well as the summer solstice. The temple's name, which means "snail," comes from a spiral staircase within the structure.

On the east side of El Caracol, a path leads north into the bush to the **Cenote Xtoloc,** a natural limestone well that provided the city's daily water supply. If you see any lizards sunning there, they may well be *xtoloc,* the species for which this *cenote* is named.

TEMPLO DE LOS TABLEROS (TEMPLE OF PANELS)   Just south of El Caracol are the ruins of a *temazcalli* (a steam bath) and the Temple of Panels, named for the carved panels on top. This temple was once covered by a much larger structure, only traces of which remain.

EDIFICIO DE LAS MONJAS (EDIFICE OF THE NUNS)   If you've visited the Puuc sites of Kabah, Sayil, Labná, or Xlapak, the enormous nunnery here will remind you of the palaces at those sites. Built in the late Classic period, the new edifice was constructed over an older one. Suspecting that this was so, Le Plongeon, an archaeologist working early in the 20th century, put dynamite between the two and blew away part of the exterior, revealing the older structures within. You can still see the results of Le Plongeon's indelicate exploratory methods.

On the east side of the Edifice of the Nuns is **Anexo Este (annex)** constructed in highly ornate Chenes style with Chaac masks and serpents.

LA IGLESIA (THE CHURCH)   Next to the annex is one of the oldest buildings at Chichén, the Church. Masks of Chaac decorate two upper stories. Look closely, and you'll see other pagan symbols among the crowd of Chaacs: an armadillo, a crab, a snail, and a tortoise. These represent the Maya gods, called *bacah,* whose job it was to hold up the sky.

AKAB DZIB (TEMPLE OF OBSCURE WRITING)   Beloved of travel writers, this temple lies east of the Edifice of the Nuns. Above a door in one of the rooms are some Mayan glyphs, which gave the temple its name because the writings have yet to be deciphered. In other rooms, traces of red handprints are still visible. Reconstructed and expanded over the centuries, Akab Dzib may be the oldest building at Chichén.

CHICHEN VIEJO (OLD CHICHEN)   For a look at more of Chichén's oldest buildings, constructed well before the time of Toltec influence, follow signs from the Edifice of the Nuns southwest into the bush to Old Chichén, about 1km (a half-mile) away. Be prepared for this trek with long trousers, insect repellent, and a local guide. The attractions here are the **Templo de los Inscripciones Iniciales (Temple of the First Inscriptions),** with the oldest inscriptions discovered at Chichén, and the restored **Templo de los Dinteles (Temple of the Lintels),** a fine Puuc building. Some of these buildings have recently undergone restoration.

WHERE TO STAY

The expensive hotels in Chichén all occupy beautiful grounds, are close to the ruins, and serve decent food. All have toll-free reservations numbers. These hotels do a lot of business with tour operators—they can be empty one day and full the next. From these hotels you can easily walk to the back entrance of the ruins, next to the Hotel Mayaland. There are several inexpensive hotels in the village of Pisté, just to the west of the ruins. There is no advantage to staying in Pisté other than the proximity to Chichén Itzá. It is an unattractive village with little to recommend it. Another option is to stay in the colonial town of Valladolid, 40 minutes away.

EXPENSIVE

Hacienda Chichén Resort *Rᴿ* This is the smallest and most private of the hotels at the ruins. It is also the quietest. This former hacienda served as the headquarters for the Carnegie Institute's excavations in 1923. Several bungalows scattered about the property were built to house the institute's staff. Each one houses one or two units. Rooms come with a dehumidifier, a ceiling fan, and good air-conditioning. The floors are ceramic tile, the ceilings are stucco with wood beams, and the walls are decorated with carved stone trim. Trees and tropical plants fill the manicured gardens. You can enjoy these from your room's porch or from the terrace restaurant, which occupies part of the original hacienda owner's house. Standard rooms come with a queen-size, two twin, or two double beds. Suites are bigger and have sitting areas with sleeper-sofas. These come with king-size beds. The main building belonged to the hacienda; it houses the terrace restaurant.

Zona Arqueológica, 97751 Chichén Itzá, Yuc. ©/fax **985/851-0045.** www.hacienda chichen.com. (Reservations: Casa del Balam, Calle 60 no. 488, 97000 Mérida, Yuc.; © 800/624-8451 in the U.S., or 999/924-2150; fax 999/924-5011.) 28 units. $175 (£96) double; $200 (£110) junior suite. AE, MC, V. Free guarded parking. **Amenities:** Restaurant; 2 bars; large outdoor pool. *In room:* A/C, minibar, hair dryer, no phone.

Hotel & Bungalows Mayaland *RᴿR* The main doorway frames El Caracol (the Observatory) in a stunning view—that's how close this hotel is to the ruins. The long main building is three stories high. The rooms are large, with comfortable beds and large tiled bathrooms. Bungalows, scattered about the rest of the grounds, are built native style, with thatched roofs and stucco walls; they're a good deal larger than the rooms. The grounds are gorgeous, with huge trees and lush foliage—the hotel has had 75 years to get them in shape. The suites are on the top floor of the main building and come with terraces and two-person Jacuzzis. The "lodge section" consists of two groupings of larger bungalows in the back of the property surrounded by a lovely garden and pool area. Rates for November, Christmas, and the spring equinox are a little higher than posted here.

Zona Arqueológica, 97751 Chichén Itzá, Yuc. ⓒ **985/851-0100.** www.mayaland. com. (Reservations: Mayaland Resorts, Robalo 30 SM3, 77500 Cancún, Q. Roo; ⓒ 800/235-4079 in the U.S., or 998/887-2495; fax 998/887-4510.) 97 units. High season $192 (£106) double, $278 (£153) bungalow, $316 (£174) suite, $438–$520 (£241–£286) lodge bungalows; low season $103 (£57) double, $168 (£92) bungalow, $230 (£127) suite, $192–$248 (£106–£136) lodge bungalows. Higher rates are for units with Jacuzzis. AE, MC, V. Free guarded parking. **Amenities:** 2 restaurants; bar; 3 outdoor pools; tour desk; room service; babysitting; laundry service. *In room:* A/C, TV, minibar, coffeemaker.

MODERATE

Villas Arqueológicas Chichén Itzá ⓐ   This hotel is built around a courtyard and a pool. Two massive royal Poinciana trees tower above the grounds, and bougainvillea drapes the walls. This chain has similar hotels at Cobá and Uxmal, and is connected with Club Med. The rooms are modern and comfortable, unless you're 1.9m (6 ft., 2 in.) or taller—each bed is in a niche, with walls at the head and foot. Most rooms have one double bed and a twin bed. You can book a half- or full-board plan or just the room.

Zona Arqueológica, 97751 Chichén Itzá, Yuc. ⓒ **800/258-2633** in the U.S., or 985/851-0034 or 985/856-2830. 40 units. $100 (£55) double. Rates include continental breakfast. Half-board (breakfast plus lunch or dinner) $18 (£9.90) per person; full board (3 meals) $35 (£19) per person. AE, MC, V. Free parking. **Amenities:** Restaurant; bar; large outdoor pool; tennis court; tour desk. *In room:* A/C, hair dryer.

INEXPENSIVE

Hotel Dolores Alba *(Value)*   This place is of the motel variety, perfect if you come by car. It is a bargain for what you get: two pools (one really special), *palapas* and hammocks around the place, and large, comfortable rooms. The restaurant serves good meals at moderate prices. There is free transportation to the ruins and the Caves of Balankanché during visiting hours, though you will have to take a taxi back. The hotel is on the highway 2.5km (1½ miles) east of the ruins (toward Valladolid). Rooms come with two double beds.

Carretera Mérida–Valladolid Km 122, Yuc. ⓒ **985/858-1555.** www.doloresalba. com. (Reservations: Hotel Dolores Alba, Calle 63 no. 464, 97000 Mérida, Yuc.; ⓒ 999/928-5650; fax 999/928-3163.) 40 units. $45 (£25) double. MC, V (8% service charge). Free parking. **Amenities:** Restaurant; bar; 2 outdoor pools; room service. *In room:* A/C, TV, no phone.

WHERE TO DINE

Although there's no great food in this area, there is plenty of decent food. The best idea is to stick to simple choices. The restaurant at the visitor center at the ruins serves decent snack food. The hotel restaurants mostly do a fair job, and, if you're in the village of Pisté, you can try one of the restaurants along the highway there that cater to the bus tours, such as **Fiesta** (© **985/851-0111**). The best time to go is early lunch or regular supper hours, when the buses are gone.

Appendix:
Useful Terms & Phrases

1 Basic Vocabulary

Most Mexicans are very patient with foreigners who try to speak their language; it helps a lot to know a few basic phrases. I've included simple phrases for expressing basic needs, followed by some common menu items.

ENGLISH-SPANISH PHRASES

English	Spanish	Pronunciation
Good day	**Buen día**	bwehn *dee*-ah
Good morning	**Buenos días**	*bweh*-nohss *dee*-ahss
How are you?	**¿Cómo está?**	*koh*-moh ehss-*tah*?
Very well	**Muy bien**	mwee byehn
Thank you	**Gracias**	*grah*-syahss
You're welcome	**De nada**	deh *nah*-dah
Good-bye	**Adiós**	ah-*dyohss*
Please	**Por favor**	pohr fah-*vohr*
Yes	**Sí**	see
No	**No**	noh
Excuse me	**Perdóneme**	pehr-*doh*-neh-meh
Give me	**Déme**	*deh*-meh
Where is . . . ?	**¿Dónde está . . . ?**	*dohn*-deh ehss-*tah*?
the station	**la estación**	lah ehss-tah-*syohn*

English	Spanish	Pronunciation
a hotel	**un hotel**	oon oh-*tehl*
a gas station	**una gasolinera**	*oo*-nah gah-soh-lee-*neh*-rah
a restaurant	**un restaurante**	oon res-tow-*rahn*-teh
the toilet	**el baño**	el *bah*-nyoh
a good doctor	**un buen médico**	oon bwehn *meh*-dee-coh
the road to . . .	**el camino a/hacia . . .**	el cah-*mee*-noh ah/*ah*-syah
To the right	**A la derecha**	ah lah deh-*reh*-chah
To the left	**A la izquierda**	ah lah ees-*kyehr*-dah
Straight ahead	**Derecho**	deh-*reh*-choh
I would like	**Quisiera**	key-*syeh*-rah
I want	**Quiero**	*kyeh*-roh
to eat	**comer**	koh-*mehr*
a room	**una habitación**	*oo*-nah ah-bee-tah-*syohn*
Do you have . . . ?	**¿Tiene usted . . . ?**	tyeh-neh oo-*sted?*
a book	**un libro**	oon *lee*-broh
a dictionary	**un diccionario**	oon deek-syow-*nah*-ryo
How much is it?	**¿Cuánto cuesta?**	*kwahn*-toh *kwehss*-tah?
When?	**¿Cuándo?**	*kwahn*-doh?
What?	**¿Qué?**	keh?
There is (Is there . . . ?)	**(¿)Hay (. . . ?)**	eye?
What is there?	**¿Qué hay?**	keh eye?
Yesterday	**Ayer**	ah-*yer*
Today	**Hoy**	oy
Tomorrow	**Mañana**	mah-*nyah*-nah
Good	**Bueno**	*bweh*-noh
Bad	**Malo**	*mah*-loh

English	Spanish	Pronunciation
Better (best)	(Lo) Mejor	(loh) meh-*hohr*
More	Más	mahs
Less	Menos	*meh*-nohss
No smoking	Se prohibe fumar	seh proh-*ee*-beh foo-*mahr*
Postcard	Tarjeta postal	tar-*heh*-ta pohs-*tahl*
Insect repellent	Repelente contra insectos	reh-peh-*lehn*-te *cohn*-trah een-*sehk*-tos

MORE USEFUL PHRASES

English	Spanish	Pronunciation
Do you speak English?	¿Habla usted inglés?	*ah*-blah oo-*sted* een-*glehs*?
Is there anyone here who speaks English?	¿Hay alguien aquí que hable inglés?	eye *ahl*-gyehn ah-*kee* keh *ah*-bleh een-*glehs*?
I speak a little Spanish.	Hablo un poco de español.	*ah*-bloh oon *poh*-koh deh ehss-pah-*nyohl*
I don't understand Spanish very well.	No (lo) entiendo muy bien el español.	noh (loh) ehn-*tyehn*-doh mwee byehn el ehss-pah-*nyohl*
The meal is good.	Me gusta la comida.	meh *goo*-stah lah koh-*mee*-dah
What time is it?	¿Qué hora es?	keh *oh*-rah ehss?
May I see your menu?	¿Puedo ver el menú (la carta)?	*pueh*-do vehr el meh-*noo* (lah *car*-tah)?
The check, please.	La cuenta, por favor.	lah *quehn*-tah pohr fa-*vorh*
What do I owe you?	¿Cuánto le debo?	*kwahn*-toh leh *deh*-boh?

English	Spanish	Pronunciation
What did you say?	¿Mande? (formal)	*mahn*-deh?
	¿Cómo? (informal)	*koh*-moh?
I want (to see) . . .	Quiero (ver) . . .	*kyeh*-roh (vehr)
a room	un cuarto or	oon *kwar*-toh,
	una habitación	*oo*-nah ah-bee-tah-*syohn*
for two persons	para dos personas.	*pah*-rah dohss pehr-*soh*-nahs
with (without) bathroom	con (sin) baño	kohn (seen) *bah*-nyoh
We are staying here only . . .	Nos quedamos aquí solamente . . .	nohs keh-*dah*-mohss ah-*kee* soh-lah-*mehn*-teh
one night.	una noche.	*oo*-nah *noh*-cheh
one week.	una semana.	*oo*-nah seh-*mah*-nah
We are leaving . . .	Partimos (Salimos) . . .	pahr-*tee*-mohss (sah-*lee*-mohss)
tomorrow.	mañana.	mah-*nya*-nah
Do you accept . . . ?	¿Acepta usted . . . ?	ah-*sehp*-tah oo-*sted*
traveler's checks?	cheques de viajero?	*cheh*-kehss deh byah-*heh*-roh?
Is there a laundromat . . . ?	¿Hay una lavandería . . . ?	eye *oo*-nah lah-*vahn*-deh-*ree*-ah
near here?	cerca de aquí?	*sehr*-kah deh ah-*kee*
Please send these clothes to the laundry.	Hágame el favor de mandar esta ropa a la lavandería.	*ah*-gah-meh el fah-*vohr* deh mahn-*dahr* *ehss*-tah *roh*-pah a lah lah-*vahn*-deh-ree-ah

NUMBERS

1	**uno** (*ooh*-noh)	17	**diecisiete** (dyess-ee-*syeh*-teh)
2	**dos** (dohss)	18	**dieciocho** (dyess-ee-*oh*-choh)
3	**tres** (trehss)	19	**diecinueve** (dyess-ee-*nweh*-beh)
4	**cuatro** (*kwah*-troh)		
5	**cinco** (*seen*-koh)	20	**veinte** (*bayn*-teh)
6	**seis** (sayss)	30	**treinta** (*trayn*-tah)
7	**siete** (*syeh*-teh)	40	**cuarenta** (kwah-*ren*-tah)
8	**ocho** (*oh*-choh)	50	**cincuenta** (seen-*kwen*-tah)
9	**nueve** (*nweh*-beh)	60	**sesenta** (seh-*sehn*-tah)
10	**diez** (dyess)	70	**setenta** (seh-*tehn*-tah)
11	**once** (*ohn*-seh)	80	**ochenta** (oh-*chehn*-tah)
12	**doce** (*doh*-seh)	90	**noventa** (noh-*behn*-tah)
13	**trece** (*treh*-seh)	100	**cien** (syehn)
14	**catorce** (kah-*tohr*-seh)	200	**doscientos** (do-*syehn*-tohs)
15	**quince** (*keen*-seh)	500	**quinientos** (kee-*nyehn*-tohs)
16	**dieciseis** (dyess-ee-*sayss*)	1,000	**mil** (meel)

TRANSPORTATION TERMS

English	Spanish	Pronunciation
Airport	**Aeropuerto**	ah-eh-roh-*pwehr*-toh
Flight	**Vuelo**	*bweh*-loh
Rental car	**Arrendadora de autos**	ah-rehn-da-doh-rah deh ow-tohs
Bus	**Autobús**	ow-toh-*boos*
Bus or truck	**Camión**	ka-*myohn*
Lane	**Carril**	kah-*reel*
Nonstop	**Directo**	dee-*rehk*-toh
Baggage (claim area)	**Equipajes**	eh-kee-*pah*-hehss
Intercity	**Foraneo**	foh-rah-*neh*-oh
Luggage storage area	**Guarda equipaje**	gwar-dah eh-kee-*pah*-heh
Arrival gates	**Llegadas**	yeh-*gah*-dahss
Originates at this station	**Local**	loh-*kahl*
Originates elsewhere	**De paso**	deh *pah*-soh

English	Spanish	Pronunciation
Stops if seats available	**Para si hay lugares**	*pah*-rah see eye loo-*gah*-rehs
First class	**Primera**	pree-*meh*-rah
Second class	**Segunda**	seh-*goon*-dah
Nonstop	**Sin escala**	seen ess-*kah*-lah
Baggage claim area	**Recibo de equipajes**	reh-see-boh deh eh-kee-*pah*-hehss
Waiting room	**Sala de espera**	*sah*-lah deh ehss-*peh*-rah
Toilets	**Sanitarios**	sah-nee-*tah*-ryohss
Ticket window	**Taquilla**	tah-*kee*-yah

2 Menu Glossary

Achiote Small red seed of the *annatto* tree.

Achiote preparado A Yucatecan prepared paste made of ground *achiote,* wheat and corn flour, cumin, cinnamon, salt, onion, garlic, and oregano.

Agua fresca Fruit-flavored water, usually watermelon, cantaloupe, chia seed with lemon, hibiscus flour, rice, or ground melon-seed mixture.

Antojito Typical Mexican supper foods, usually made with *masa* or tortillas and having a filling or topping such as sausage, cheese, beans, and onions; includes such things as tacos, tostadas, *sopes,* and *garnachas.*

Atole A thick, lightly sweet, hot drink made with finely ground corn and usually flavored with vanilla, pecan, strawberry, pineapple, or chocolate.

Botana An appetizer.

Buñuelos Round, thin, deep-fried crispy fritters dipped in sugar.

Carnitas Pork deep-cooked (not fried) in lard, and then simmered and served with corn tortillas for tacos.

Ceviche Fresh raw seafood marinated in fresh lime juice and garnished with chopped tomatoes, onions, chiles, and sometimes cilantro.

Chayote A vegetable pear or mirliton, a type of spiny squash boiled and served as an accompaniment to meat dishes.

Chiles en nogada Poblano peppers stuffed with a mixture of ground pork and beef, spices, fruits, raisins, and almonds. Can be served either warm—fried in a light batter—or cold, sans the batter. Either way it is then covered in walnut-and-cream sauce.

Chiles rellenos Usually poblano peppers stuffed with cheese or spicy ground meat with raisins, rolled in a batter, and fried.

Churro Tube-shaped, breadlike fritter, dipped in sugar and some-times filled with *cajeta* (milk-based caramel) or chocolate.

Cochinita pibil Pork wrapped in banana leaves, pit-baked in a *pibil* sauce of *achiote,* sour orange, and spices; common in the Yucatán.

Enchilada A tortilla dipped in sauce, usually filled with chicken or white cheese, and sometimes topped with mole (*enchiladas rojas* or *de mole*), or with tomato sauce and sour cream (*enchiladas suizas*—Swiss enchiladas), or covered in a green sauce *(enchiladas verdes),* or topped with onions, sour cream, and guacamole *(enchiladas potosinas).*

Escabeche A lightly pickled sauce used in Yucatecan chicken stew.

Frijoles refritos Pinto beans mashed and cooked with lard.

Garnachas A thickish small circle of fried *masa* with pinched sides, topped with pork or chicken, onions, and avocado, or some-times chopped potatoes and tomatoes, typical as a *botana* in Vera-cruz and the Yucatán.

Gorditas Thick, fried corn tortillas, slit and stuffed with choice of cheese, beans, beef, chicken, with or without lettuce, tomato, and onion garnish.

Horchata Refreshing drink made of ground rice or melon seeds, ground almonds, cinnamon, and lightly sweetened.

Huevos mexicanos Scrambled eggs with chopped onions, hot green peppers, and tomatoes.

Huitlacoche Sometimes spelled "cuitlacoche." A mushroom-flavored black fungus that appears on corn in the rainy season; con-sidered a delicacy.

Manchamantel Translated, means "tablecloth stainer." A stew of chicken or pork with chiles, tomatoes, pineapple, bananas, and jicama.

Masa Ground corn soaked in lime; the basis for tamales, corn tor-tillas, and soups.

Mixiote Rabbit, lamb, or chicken cooked in a mild chile sauce (usually chile *ancho* or *pasilla*), and then wrapped like a tamal and steamed. It is generally served with tortillas for tacos, with traditional garnishes of pickled onions, hot sauce, chopped cilantro, and lime wedges.

Pan de muerto   Sweet bread made around the Days of the Dead (Nov 1–2), in the form of mummies or dolls, or round with bone designs.

Pan dulce   Lightly sweetened bread in many configurations, usually served at breakfast or bought in any bakery.

Papadzules   Tortillas stuffed with hard-boiled eggs and seeds (pumpkin or sunflower) in a tomato sauce.

Pibil   Pit-baked pork or chicken in a sauce of tomato, onion, mild red pepper, cilantro, and vinegar.

Pipián   A sauce made with ground pumpkin seeds, nuts, and mild peppers.

Poc chuc   Slices of pork with onion marinated in a tangy sour orange sauce and charcoal-broiled; a Yucatecan specialty.

Pozole   A soup made with hominy in either chicken or pork broth.

Pulque   A drink made of fermented juice of the maguey plant; best in the state of Hidalgo and around Mexico City.

Quesadilla   Corn or flour tortillas stuffed with melted white cheese and lightly fried.

Queso relleno   "Stuffed cheese," a mild yellow cheese stuffed with minced meat and spices; a Yucatecan specialty.

Rompope   Delicious Mexican eggnog, invented in Puebla, made with eggs, vanilla, sugar, and rum.

Salsa verde   An uncooked sauce using the green tomatillo and puréed with spicy or mild hot peppers, onions, garlic, and cilantro; on tables countrywide.

Sopa de flor de calabaza   A soup made of chopped squash or pumpkin blossoms.

Sopa de lima   A tangy soup made with chicken broth and accented with fresh lime; popular in the Yucatán.

Sopa de tortilla   A traditional chicken broth–based soup, seasoned with chiles, tomatoes, onion, and garlic, served with crispy fried strips of corn tortillas.

Sopa tlalpeña (or *caldo tlalpeño*)   A hearty soup made with chunks of chicken, chopped carrots, zucchini, corn, onions, garlic, and cilantro.

Sopa tlaxcalteca   A hearty tomato-based soup filled with cooked *nopal* cactus, cheese, cream, and avocado, with crispy tortilla strips floating on top.

Sope   Pronounced "*soh*-peh." An *antojito* similar to a *garnacha,* except spread with refried beans and topped with crumbled cheese and onions.

Tacos al pastor   Thin slices of flavored pork roasted on a revolving cylinder dripping with onion slices and juice of fresh pineapple slices. Served in small corn tortillas, topped with chopped onion and cilantro.

Tamal   Incorrectly called a tamale (*tamal* singular, *tamales* plural). A meat or sweet filling rolled with fresh *masa,* wrapped in a corn husk or banana leaf, and steamed.

Tikin xic   Also seen on menus as "tik-n-xic" and "tikik chick." Charbroiled fish brushed with *achiote* sauce.

Torta   A sandwich, usually on *bolillo* bread, typically with sliced avocado, onions, tomatoes, with a choice of meat and often cheese.

Xtabentun   Pronounced "shtah-behn-*toon.*" A Yucatecan liquor made of fermented honey and flavored with anise. It comes *seco* (dry) or *crema* (sweet).

Zacahuil   Pork leg tamal, packed in thick *masa,* wrapped in banana leaves, and pit-baked, sometimes pot-made with tomato and *masa;* a specialty of mid- to upper Veracruz.

Index

See also Accommodations and Restaurant indexes below.

ACCOMMODATIONS

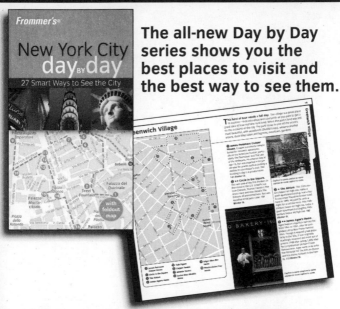

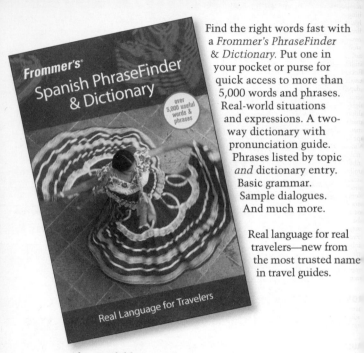

FROMMER'S® CRUISE GUIDES

Alaska Cruises & Ports of Call

Cruises & Ports of Call

European Cruises & Ports of Call

FROMMER'S® NATIONAL PARK GUIDES

Algonquin Provincial Park
Banff & Jasper
Grand Canyon

National Parks of the American West
Rocky Mountain
Yellowstone & Grand Teton

Yosemite and Sequoia & Kings
Canyon
Zion & Bryce Canyon

FROMMER'S® MEMORABLE WALKS

London
New York

Paris
Rome

San Francisco

FROMMER'S® WITH KIDS GUIDES

Chicago
Hawaii
Las Vegas
London

National Parks
New York City
San Francisco

Toronto
Walt Disney World® & Orlando
Washington, D.C.

SUZY GERSHMAN'S BORN TO SHOP GUIDES

France
Hong Kong, Shanghai & Beijing
Italy

London
New York

Paris
San Francisco

FROMMER'S® IRREVERENT GUIDES

Amsterdam
Boston
Chicago
Las Vegas

London
Los Angeles
Manhattan
Paris

Rome
San Francisco
Walt Disney World®
Washington, D.C.

FROMMER'S® BEST-LOVED DRIVING TOURS

Austria
Britain
California
France

Germany
Ireland
Italy
New England

Northern Italy
Scotland
Spain
Tuscany & Umbria

THE UNOFFICIAL GUIDES®

Adventure Travel in Alaska
Beyond Disney
California with Kids
Central Italy
Chicago
Cruises
Disneyland®
England
Florida
Florida with Kids

Hawaii
Ireland
Las Vegas
London
Maui
Mexico's Best Beach Resorts
Mini Mickey
New Orleans
New York City

Paris
San Francisco
South Florida including Miami &
the Keys
Walt Disney World®
Walt Disney World® for
Grown-ups
Walt Disney World® with Kids
Washington, D.C.

SPECIAL-INTEREST TITLES

Athens Past & Present
Best Places to Raise Your Family
Cities Ranked & Rated
500 Places to Take Your Kids Before They Grow Up
Frommer's Best Day Trips from London
Frommer's Best RV & Tent Campgrounds
in the U.S.A.

Frommer's Exploring America by RV
Frommer's NYC Free & Dirt Cheap
Frommer's Road Atlas Europe
Frommer's Road Atlas Ireland
Great Escapes From NYC Without Wheels
Retirement Places Rated

FROMMER'S® PHRASEFINDER DICTIONARY GUIDES

French

Italian

Spanish

CLOSED
due to
accidental demolition

WEGEN BISSIGEN
EICHHÖRNCHEN GESCHLOSSEN

CERRADO
CABRAS

Κλειστό
Μετεωρίτες

POOL CLOSED
プール も
ELECTRIC EELS
閉鎖中

Hotel
closed for
facelifting

FERMÉ POUR
RAISON
DE GRÈVE
DES BONNES

FECHADO!
POR CAUSA DE
ATAQUES DOS CROCODILOS

I don't speak
sign language.

A hotel can close for all kinds of reasons.
Our Guarantee ensures that if your hotel's undergoing construction,
we'll let you know in advance. In fact, we cover your entire travel
experience. See www.travelocity.com/guarantee for details.

travelocity
You'll never roam alone.

There's a parking lot where my ocean view should be.

 À la place de la vue sur l'océan, me voilà avec une vue sur un parking.

 Anstatt Meerblick habe ich Sicht auf einen Parkplatz.

 Al posto della vista sull'oceano c'è un parcheggio.

 No tengo vista al mar porque hay un parque de estacionamiento.

 Há um parque de estacionamento onde deveria estar a minha vista do ocean

 Ett parkeringsområde har byggts på den plats där min utsikt över oceanen borde vara.

 Er ligt een parkeerterrein waar mijn zee-uitzicht zou moeten zijn.

 هنالك موقف للسيارات مكان ما وجب ان يكون المنظر الخلاب المطل على المحيط .

 眼前に広がる紺碧の海・・・じゃない。窓の外は駐車場

 停车场的位置应该是我的海景所在。

— I'm fluent in pig latin.

Hotel mishaps aren't bound by geography.
Neither is our Guarantee. It covers your entire travel experience,
including the price. So if you don't get the ocean view you
booked, we'll work with our travel partners to make it right,
right away. See Travelocity.com/guarantee for details.

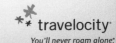
travelocity
You'll never roam alone.